DISCOVER THE
POCONOS
WITH
KIDS

A Guide for Families

DISCOVER THE
POCONOS
WITH
KIDS

A Guide for Families

Marynell K. Strunk

Discover the Poconos with Kids
First Edition
© 1998 by Marynell Strunk

ISBN 1-881409-20-1

Cover design: Mike Jaynes and Marge Mueller
Cover and frontispiece photos courtesy Pocono Mountains Vacation Bureau, Inc.
Production, typesetting, and layout by Gray Mouse Graphics
Map by Gray Mouse Graphics
Photos by the author unless otherwise noted.
Frontispiece: Capture family memories on your outing in the Poconos. Photo courtesy Pocono Mountains Visitors Bureau

JASI Post Office Box 313
Medina, Washington 98039
(425) 454-3490; FAX: (425) 462-1335; e-mail jasibooks@aol.com

Printed in the United States of America

Library of Congress Cataloging-in-Publication Data

Strunk, Marynell K., 1962–
Discover the Poconos with kids : a guide for families / Marynell K. Strunk.
p. cm.
Includes bibliographical references and index.
ISBN 1-881409-20-1
1. Pocono Mountain (Pa.)--Guidebooks. 2. Family recreation--Pennsylvania--Pocono Mountains--Guidebooks. I. Title.
F157.M6S87 1998
917.48'20443--dc21   97-44471
      CIP

This book is dedicated to my family:

*David, Kelly, Morgan, Mackenzie,
and my mother, Mary.*

• • •

*They are my source for love, strength, support,
and adventure.*

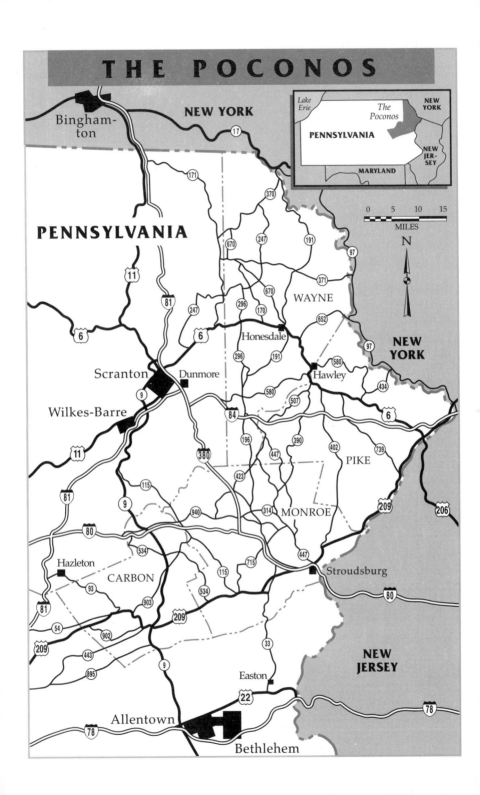

THE POCONOS

TABLE OF CONTENTS

· ·

Foreword: Robert Uguccioni 9

Acknowledgments 10

Introduction 11

Before You Start 13
    Activity Codes 13
    Transportation 13
    Helpful Phone Numbers 14
    Travel Tips for Families 14
    Pocono Region Tourism Contacts 15

Chapter 1: Family Resorts and Campgrounds 17
    Country Inns, Cottages, and Resorts 17
    Time-sharing and Vacation Home Rental Options 27
    Campgrounds 28

Chapter 2: Animals 35

Chapter 3: Demonstrations 41

Chapter 4: History 45

Chapter 5: Festivals and Celebrations 57

Chapter 6: Libraries 67

Chapter 7: Movies 73

Chapter 8: Museums 75

Chapter 9: Nature 85
    Environmental Education Centers 85
    Wildlife Rehabilitation Centers 89

National and State Park Nature Programs 91
Harvesting 92

Chapter 10: Parks 97
State and National Parks 97
Amusement Parks 101

Chapter 11: Performing Arts 109
Music 109
Television 113
Theater 113

Chapter 12: Sports... 117
Bicycling 117
Boating, Canoeing, and Rafting 121
Bowling 128
Fishing 129
Horseback Riding 130
Miniature Golf 132
Skiing 134
Ice Skating 140
Roller Skating, In-Line Skating, and Skateboarding ... 142
Spectator Sports 144
Swimming 148

Chapter 13: Tours 151
Air 151
Boat 152
Bus 154
Railroad 154
Trolley 156
Guided or Self-Guided Tours 157
The World of Work 160

Recommended Reading List 162

Quick Guide to Activities 164

Index 171

FOREWORD

Having raised my own children here in the Pocono Mountains, I know from firsthand experience the wealth of family-friendly activities and places to be found here. Our Pocono Region is a place where kids of all ages can be kids, where young minds and bodies can grow strong (and tired, if you're lucky!).

Families—both visitors and residents—have been enjoying the Pocono Mountains since the 1800s. With 2,400 square miles of attractions, parks, lakes, streams, and rivers to enjoy, there is something to suit every family's budget and taste. Using *Discover the Poconos with Kids*, you can explore every inch of the Poconos, be it Carbon, Monroe, Pike or Wayne County. You and your family—and your visitors—can plan a day, a weekend or a whole vacation using this excellent book.

I hope you take advantage of all there is to do and see in our beautiful region.

Your Friend in the Poconos,

Robert Uguccioni

Robert Uguccioni, Executive Director
Pocono Mountains Vacation Bureau, Inc.

ACKNOWLEDGMENTS

· ·

As with any undertaking, the final product is usually the result of a team effort. I want to thank the people who made the experience a little less overwhelming.

My two little girls, Kelly and Mackenzie, are directly responsible for the concept of this book. They were also very willing participants with the research. My dear friend Brenda Friday for extending much needed encouragement during the ups and downs as well as assisting with the editing of the manuscript. My mother, Mary Kelly, for her ability to step in and help out when it was needed. Elisabeth Gephart and Harry Roach for voices of experience during the idea stage. Robert Uguccioni, Kristine Petersen, and Jennifer Call at the Pocono Mountain Vacation Bureau for their knowledge, support, and generosity with time and materials. Jim Brunkard and the Fine Arts Discovery Series for providing me with information and materials.

Last but not least, to my beloved husband, whose love and support was unwavering.

Again, thank you.

INTRODUCTION

. . . .

I hope all the readers of this guidebook have as much fun using this book as I had researching and writing it. As the Poconos first family guidebook, residents and visitors alike will now be able to flip through the pages and plan an awesome day, rain or shine, with the children.

I have made efforts to include the obvious as well as the not-so-obvious attractions the Poconos offer to help plan that extra special day. I have also included activities that can be shared with a physically-challenged child and made an index specifically for this category. Other indexes reference rainy day activities, birthday party facilities, places that welcome school groups, as well as an index of free things to do.

All the selections in this book are things that are intended to be done *with* your child, a special child you know, a grandchild, or *with* a group of children. Nothing is more satisfying than exposing a young mind to the wonders of the world. Picking fresh strawberries, petting an animal, or browsing through an art gallery can be extra special when shared with the special little people in your life. The age appropriateness of an activity should be taken into consideration by the adult in charge. If you have any concerns, call ahead.

The logistics of traveling with children can sometimes be interesting. Therefore, please read the next section, Before You Start, with helpful phone numbers and travel tips. Be prepared; unplanned chaos is always looming.

In addition to activities in the Pocono region, I have also listed special attractions located in the nearby Lehigh Valley and the Scranton/Wilkes-Barre areas. If you plan to visit any of the places listed, it is strongly recommended that you call first. If you are taking a large group, be sure to inquire about group rates. Prices and hours of operation are subject to change at any time without notice.

In addition, if there is a place that is not listed in this book, and could be, please contact me with the name, address, and phone number. I would love to investigate it and include it in the next edition. I would also like readers to share any comments. Please write to me at: JASI, PO Box 313, Medina, WA 98039. E-mail inquiries may be sent to jasibooks@aol.com.

Enjoy your adventure and happy traveling!

Marynell K. Strunk

BEFORE YOU START

• •

ACTIVITY CODES

🎂 = Birthday Party Facilities

Ⓢ = Free

👫 = Group Rates/School Group

♿ = Wheelchair and Stroller Accessibility

☂ = Rainy Day Activities

TRANSPORTATION
Air

Lehigh Valley International Airport	(610) 266-6000
Allentown, PA	
Newark International Airport	(201) 961-4750
Newark, NJ	
Philadelphia International Airport	(215) 937-8937
Philadelphia, PA	
Pocono Mountain Municipal Airport	(717) 829-6980
Mount Pocono, PA	
Stroudsburg/Pocono Airport	(717) 421-8900
East Stroudsburg, PA	
Wilkes-Barre/Scranton International	(717) 457-3445
Avoca, PA	

Bus

Martz Trailways (provides daily service to and from New York City)	(717) 421-3040
Monroe County Transit Authority (provides local service)	(717) 424-9500

Taxi

TICA Bus and Taxi (717) 421-6068

HELPFUL PHONE NUMBERS

All Emergencies	911
Child Abuse Hot Line (Monroe County only)	(717) 420-3590
Fall Foliage Hot Line	(717) 421-5565
Local Weather	(717) 476-5465, ext. 1039
Poison Control Center	(800) 722-7112
Pocono Medical Center	(717) 421-4000
Pocono Ski Report	(717) 421-5565
Pennsylvania Game Commission	(800) 228-0789
Pennsylvania Fish and Boat Commission,	
Northeastern Pennsylvania Office	(717) 657-4518
(boat registration)	(717) 657-4551, (717) 477-5717
Traveler's Information Radio Station	530AM*

*Within a 10-mile radius of Delaware Water Gap, Pennsylvania, you will be able to get current information on Pocono events.

TRAVEL TIPS FOR FAMILIES

Call Before You Go: Despite the painstaking work I have done to get current and accurate information for this book, hours of operation change, prices go up, and places close without notice. You can safeguard yourself against such surprises by calling ahead. By contacting the place by either mail or phone you can also get an even better idea of what to expect.

Pack Snacks: It is always a good idea to pack some easy to eat food and drinks. It saves time, money, and sometimes your sanity.

Bring Extra Clothes: Depending on your activity and your child, an extra set of clothes can be a life saver. Remember, kids can turn a stroll along a stream into a bath.

Plan Ahead: The more you anticipate possible needs for the outing, the more fun you and the family will have on the adventure. If you are going on a hike in the middle of the summer, bug spray might be a good idea. If you are fishing, make sure you have the appropriate licenses. Call to get the local weather forecast at (717) 476-5465, ext. 1039, or refer to the local paper.

Schedule Time: The rule of thumb in this department is to consider everyone's pace and interest. If you go to a museum filled with Indian artifacts with a 2 year old, don't expect to spend the day there. Nor do you want to go to a playground and spend 10 minutes. If you're planning a tour, call ahead and see how long it lasts. For everyone to have a good time, determine the amount of time you plan to spend and coordinate the outing around mealtimes, naptimes, and interests.

Consider the Age of the Children: No one will have fun on a family outing if the kids aren't. Therefore consider the ages of the kids in your group.

Idle-Time Activities: I Spy, the License Plate Game, and Twenty Questions were invented for a reason. If your time in the car will be long or there is a possibility of waiting in line for extended periods, invest in a book of travel games or check one out of the library.

Call Before You Go: This is worth mentioning again because it's really important!

POCONO REGION TOURISM CONTACTS

Bethlehem Visitors Center	(800) 360-8687
52 West Broad Street	(610) 868-1513
Bethlehem, PA 18018-5775	www.bethour.org
Carbon County Tourist Promotion Agency	(717) 325-3673
PO Box 90	(888) JIM-THORPE
Jim Thorpe, PA 18229	
Lehigh Valley Convention and	
Visitors Bureau, Inc.	(800) 747-0561 (U.S. only)
PO Box 20785	(610) 882-9200
Lehigh Valley, PA 18002-0785	www.regiononline.com
	www.travelfile.com/get?lvcvb
Pennsylvania Northeast Territory	
Visitors Bureau	(800) 245-7711 (U.S. only)
Airport Aviation Center	(717) 457-1320
201 Hangor Road, Suite 203	www.visitnepa.org
Avoca, PA 18641	
Pocono Mountains Vacation Bureau	(800) 762-6667 (U.S. only)
1004 Main Street	(717) 424-6050
Stroudsburg, PA 18360	www.poconos.org

The many campgrounds that border on lakes and rivers make it easy for boating and swimming. Photo courtesy Pocono Mountains Vacation Bureau, Inc.

CHAPTER
1

FAMILY RESORTS AND CAMPGROUNDS

• •

Determining where you'll stay on your visit to the Poconos is one of the most important decisions you'll have to make. There are many factors to consider: amenities, price, meals, and location, to name a few. An abundance of accommodations is available throughout the four-county Pocono region. The places selected for this chapter are family-oriented and vary in price to fit all family budgets. Country inns, cottages, resorts, and time-sharing are all popular options with families who visit the Poconos.

Another very popular and fun way to see the area is to camp, although camping is a rather informal way to travel. In addition to the campsites at the national and state parks in the Pocono region, private campgrounds offer an affordable alternative. Campgrounds are listed with the information needed to help you decide which one is right for you. Reservations are strongly recommended. Many of the campgrounds are booked a year in advance for holiday weekends.

COUNTRY INNS, COTTAGES, AND RESORTS

Rates vary depending on the season and the day of week. The rates below are based on double adult occupancy. Generally speaking child rates are slightly less expensive, depending on the age of the child. Some places may even allow children to stay free! Inquire about crib availability and charge when you call to make arrangements.

Price Codes (Based on Double Occupancy)

$	=	$0–$75 per day
$$	=	$76–$100 per day
$$$	=	$101–$150 per day
$$$$	=	$151 and up per day

Country Inns

Double W Ranch Bed and Breakfast   (717) 226-3118
RR #2, Box 1540
Honesdale, PA 18431   *$$$*

The 180-acre year-round facility is a dream come true for the horseback riding enthusiasts in your family. The ranch rustles up a great breakfast for all the cowpokes before sending you out for a day on the range. Customized packages, which include horseback riding, are available for families or large groups. The ranch provides an instructor to accompany your group so you can really ride. Depending on the season, arrangements can also be made for hay or sleigh rides. Hiking and fishing are available on-site and nearby. This secluded mountain retreat is the only dude ranch in the northeast metropolitan area.

Memorytown   (717) 839-1680
Grange Road
Mount Pocono, PA 18344   *$$*

Families have their choice of either a room at the on-site historic inn or at a private cottage set near the lake. Fishing, paddleboats, hiking, and a children's play area are available. Memorytown is also located right next to Apple Tree Farm. Apple Tree Farm offers train rides, wagon rides, a petting zoo, and more. Refer to Chapter 2 for more information on the farm.

[handwritten: Delux suite 175, 158, 149 w/ brkfst + dinner 199 per wy, 229, Victorian country]

Sterling Inn

Route 191
South Sterling, PA 18460

(717) 676-3311
(800) 523-8200
$$$$

A country inn for all seasons. On-site boating, fishing, swimming, tennis, ice skating, cross-country skiing, and more are offered at this winning resort. Packages are available to suit your tastes and schedule. As a guest, you will be able to enjoy the nature trails that weave in and around the property. Enjoy a picnic lunch prepared by the staff for your family hike. Families may choose from 56 accommodations including single rooms and individual cottages.

Cottages

Cottages provide an affordable way for families to vacation in the country. Housekeeping cottages provide beds and fully-equipped kitchens. Linens and food are usually not provided. Reservations are generally on a weekly basis. Please inquire about amenities when calling for information.

Bunnell's Pond Resort

(717) 253-2655

587 Cliff Road
Honesdale, PA 18431

$

This 54-acre getaway is open from mid-May to mid-October. Lake-front cottages provide two bedrooms, a living room, cable TV, and a kitchen equipped with utensils. Porches on all cottages include lawn chairs and picnic tables. There is free boating and fishing (in season) on the 30-acre stocked lake. A 120-foot waterfall and a swimming area will keep you cool on hot summer days.

Burney's Cottages and Motel

(717) 992-4756

HCR #1, Box 510
Sciota, PA 18354

$$

Set back off of Route 209, you can enjoy the peace and beauty of the Pocono Mountains. This year-round family paradise includes miniature golf, swings, pool, and playground. Facilities range from a one-bedroom cabin to a larger two-bedroom cabin.

Naomi Village

(717) 595-2432
(800) 33-NAOMI

PO Box 609, Route 390
Mountainhome, PA 18342

$$ – $$$$

This four-season retreat is a great place to have your next family reunion. There are a variety of accommodations to choose from. All include fully-equipped kitchens, modern baths, and bed linens. Tennis, basketball, an outdoor pool, a playground, and a fishing pond are available in a relaxing mountain setting.

Nemanie Village, Inc.

(714) 226-4518
(717) 857-0222

PO Box 77
Hawley, PA 18428

$$ – $$$$

Open from mid-May to mid-October, Nemanie Village requires a minimum stay of one week during the summer. Weekend stays are available May, June, September, and October. The individual housekeeping cottages have fully-equipped kitchens, baths, and living rooms with TV. This facility is located on Lake Wallenpaupack (Pennsylvania' s largest man-made lake). Boat slips are available as well as a private beach on the lake.

The Poconos are great for fun or relaxation. Photo by Eileen Snyder.

Resorts

Chateau at Camelback
(717) 629-5900

300 Camelback Road   *(800) 245-5900*
Tannersville, PA 18372   *$ – $$$*

"Stay and play" is the motto at the Chateau. The Chateau at Camelback is located right next to Camelback Mountain. Camelback Mountain is a first-rate ski resort in the winter, and a play and water park in the summer. Enjoy the convenience of its location and the added bonus of kids under 12 eating free. Custom packages are available year-round.

Daniels Chestnut Grove Resort
(717) 839-3656

PO Box 490, Carlton Road
Swiftwater, PA 18370-0490   *$$$*

This resort has been a family vacation spot for over 50 years. All accommodations are suitable for families. Choose from poolside, lakeside, vista, or main lodge locations. Rates include two meals per day. Your family will enjoy the indoor pool in the winter and the outdoor pool on hot summer days. Playground, tennis, game room, volleyball, basketball, archery, softball, hiking, and special planned events all add up to family fun.

Daniels Top-o-the-Poconos Resort
(717) 595-7531

PO Box 10, Route 447 North   *(800) 755-0300*
Canadensis, PA 18325   *$$*

Relax in and enjoy over 80 acres when staying at this family Pocono resort. Looking over the activity and sport schedule, there is something here to suit everyone's taste. Delaware River rafting, arts and crafts, kid's softball, and kid's movie night are just samples of the planned activities to select. There are three outdoor pools, an indoor pool, tennis, playgrounds, a fishing lake, and trout streams. Two meals are included in the daily rates along with numerous lodging options to choose from. Babysitting is also available.

[handwritten notes: 3 night special 195 per add. 80$ per child. 6 meals dinner + b. dinner style motel]

Enjoy the many natural amenities family resorts provide. Photo courtesy Pocono Mountains Vacation Bureau, Inc.

Hotel or Villa *$209 for Cts $273.48 King size* *2 $129*

Fernwood Resort (717) 588-9500

Business Route 209 (800) 233-8103
Bushkill, PA 18324 $ – $$$

Numerous year-round packages are available to fit your family's budget. Children 17 and under stay free when staying in the same room with two adults. This popular Pocono resort offers numerous on-site amenities including indoor/outdoor tennis, indoor/outdoor pools, golf course, health club, and in-season boating, fishing, horseback riding, sledding, and snowmobiling. Babysitting is available on-site so adults may enjoy a night of live entertainment. Two meals at any of the six on-site dining facilities are included in packages. When you call for information, ask about the planned activities and the Kid's Cub Club.

Hillside Lodge (717) 595-7551

PO Box 268, Route 390 (800) 666-4455
Canadensis, PA 18325 *silo.com/poconos/hillside.htm*
e-mail: dkline@postoffice.ptd.net
$$$ – $$$$

Families will have fun winter, spring, summer, and fall. Special activities are planned throughout the year with families in mind. Cross-country skiing and sledding are favorites in the winter. Summer offers poolside fun and planned group or individual activities. The playground, miniature golf, hiking nature trails, and fishing are some favorites. Pick from the numerous accommodations and packages offered.

Mountain Laurel Resort (717) 443-8411

PO Box 126 (800) 458-5921
White Haven, PA 18661 *www.mountainlaurelresort.com*
e-mail: info@mountainlaurelresort.com
$$$ – $$$$

This resort accommodates the needs of both child and adult. The unique "Leave the Kids with Us" program assures that the kids are having fun while the parents are getting that well-deserved break. The second-to-none kids' program offers an array of age-appropriate activities from ice cream making to scavenger hunts, from story hours to nature hikes. Even the family pet is allowed to join in the fun. Golf, tennis courts, indoor and outdoor pools, hiking trails, a fitness center, and fine dining are all available. Children 12 and under can stay free at a rate of one child per paying adult.

Pocmont Resort and Conference Center *(717) 588-6671*

Bushkill Falls Road   *(800) 762-6668*
Bushkill, PA 18324   *www.pocmont.com*
                                        e-mail: Pocmont@sunlink.net
                                                                $$ – $$$$

You may choose many different accommodations with packages that allow one child age 15 or under to stay and eat free. Pocmont also offers children ages 3 to 17 the use of Kids World. Kids World provides age appropriate planned activities supervised by trained counselors. On-site activities for everyone include a lake with paddle boats and rowboats, hiking trails, basketball, a game room, and indoor and outdoor pools. Winter activities include skiing at the nearby resorts, sledding, and ice skating (bring your own skates).

Shawnee Inn and Golf Resort *(800) SHAWNEE, ext. 1413*

River Road   *(717) 421-1500, ext. 1413*
Shawnee on Delaware, PA 18356   *www.shawneeinn.com*
                                                                  $$ – $$$

Positioned directly on the Delaware River, this resort offers a great deal of family fun. Swimming, skiing, roller skating, and children's theater in the summer are either on-site or nearby the resort. Shawnee Inn is also host to many of the local festivals. The Autumn Balloon Festival is a great time and beautiful sight to see on a crisp autumn day in the Poconos. Children 18 and younger stay free with a paying adult. There are also special meal plans for children. Inquire when calling for information.

The Silver Britches Lakeside Resort *(717) 226-4388*

HC 6, Box 6275
Hawley, PA 18428   *$$*

For over 50 years, the Silver Britches Lakeside Resort has been making family time special for those who choose to vacation on Lake Wallenpaupack. Situated at the widest point of the lake, guests have easy access to the shoreline with no roads to cross. Accommodations range from motel units and suites to housekeeping cottages. Meal plans are available. Watersports are the most popular activities, including water-skiing, fishing, paddle boating, rowboating, and canoeing. There is a wading pool as well as a regular pool so everyone in the family can stay cool and have fun.

Skytop Lodge

(717) 595-7401

1 Skytop, Route 390   (800) 422-7SKY
Skytop, PA 18357   www.skytop.com
e-mail: SKYTOP@PTD.NET
$$$$

One of the Poconos most exclusive and oldest resorts, Skytop occupies over 5,500 acres. The on-staff naturalist conducts nature activities year-round geared toward the entire family. Skytop hosts a supervised recreation program for children ages 3 to 12 in July and August called "Camp in the Clouds." There is a special family plan including three meals per day, and children under 16 stay free in their parents' room. A maximum of two children and a minimal service charge per child per night applies. Additional children generate some additional charges. Every April, Skytop celebrates Family Month by hosting special events and activities. Additional on-site amenities include a golf course, tennis, lawn bowling, croquet, hiking trails, biking, boating, fishing, a bathing beach, and outdoor and indoor pools. Special winter fun activities include a protected ice skating rink.

Split Rock Lodge and Conference Center

(717) 722-9111

Route 903   (800) 255-7625
Lake Harmony, PA 18624   www.splitrockresort.com
e-mail: srinfo@ptdprolog.net
$$$ – $$$$

Split Rock Lodge was originally developed as a fishing and hunting retreat and has now expanded to a four-season, full amenity resort. Accommodations range from suites and lodge rooms to villas with full kitchens and cottages. Many packages are available to cater to all tastes and pocketbooks. Children 4 and under are free. There are special rates for children 5 through 15. Planned activities for children are available. Split Rock Resort shares its fame with its neighbor, Big Boulder Ski Area. On-site amenities are numerous and include pools, tennis courts, a movie theater, golf course, children's play area, a hiking trail to the nearby state park, water sports, and a lot more. Some of these amenities require an extra charge.

Woodloch Pines

(717) 685-7121

RR#1, Box 280
Hawley, PA 18428

(800) 572-6658
www.woodloch.com
e-mail: woodmark@woodlock.com
$$ – $$$$

Woodloch Pines is a family-run resort operated with families in mind. Every day is made extra special if you stay at this Pocono resort. Accommodations range from cozy cabin rooms to spacious town houses. Babysitting is available for children if parents want to enjoy the nightlife offered. Planned activities for the young and the young-at-heart are always available as well as opportunities to relax and enjoy the mix of lakeside and wooded fun. Oktoberfest Weekend, Old Fashioned Christmas Weekend, and Peter Cottontail Weekend are a sampling of the special packages you will get to choose from.

Play areas at many of the resorts and campgounds keep kids happy for hours.

TIME-SHARING AND VACATION HOME RENTAL OPTIONS

Time-sharing and vacation home rentals are very popular options when choosing accommodations for a visit to the Poconos. Having a place of your own offers flexibility (a *must* for families). The majority of the facilities rented are equipped with kitchens, baths, and laundry, and they can sleep small or large groups under one roof. These places also come with the added benefit of having access to the amenities associated with the rental. Shuttles are provided to get you to and fro. Prices vary, depending upon size of the unit and the season. The two main time-share and vacation home rental providers in the Poconos are listed below.

Time-sharing

Shawnee VillaShare   *(717) 424-1300*

River Road
Shawnee-on-Delaware, PA 18356

Amenities Available: Shawnee Inn

The Villas at Tree Tops and Fairway   *(717) 588-9451*

Route 209
Bushkill, PA 18324

Amenities Available: Fernwood Resort

Vacation Home Rental

Fairway Villas   *(800) 343-8676*

Route 209
Bushkill, PA 18324

Amenities Available: Fernwood Resort

Shawnee's Northslope/Valley View/
Shawnee Villas   *(800) 742-9633, ext. 8970*
(717) 424-1300

PO Box 178
River Road
Shawnee-on-Delaware, PA 18356

Amenities Available: Shawnee Inn

CAMPGROUNDS

Chestnut Lake Campground
(717) 992-6179

PO Box 390
Frantz Road
Brodheadsville, PA 18322

Season: May to October
Facilities: RV, tent, water, electricity, sewage, dump station, flush toilets, telephone, showers
Amenities: Store, picnic tables, fire ring
Activities: Swimming, boating, boat rental, fishing, recreation hall, playground

Camping is great family fun, and a wonderful way to enjoy the natural surroundings of the Pocono region. Photo courtesy Pocono Mountains Vacation Bureau, Inc.

Cranberry Run Campground   *(800) 233-8240*

PO Box 309   *(717) 421-3811*
Analomink, PA 18320

Season: April to October
Facilities: RV, tent, water, electricity, sewage, dump station, flush toilets, telephone, showers
Amenities: Store, picnic tables, grills
Activities: Hiking, boating, boat rental, fishing, recreation hall, playground

Delaware Water Gap KOA   *(717) 223-8000*

RD #6, Box 6196
Hollow Road
East Stroudsburg, PA 18301

Season: April to October
Facilities: RV, tent, water, electricity, dump station, flush toilets, telephone, showers
Amenities: Store, picnic tables, fire ring
Activities: Swimming, recreation hall, playground

Dingmans Campground   *(717) 828-2266*

RR #2, Box 20, Route 209
Dingmans Ferry, PA 18328

Season: April to October
Facilities: RV, tent, water, electricity, dump station, flush toilets, pit toilets, telephone, showers
Amenities: Store, picnic tables, fire ring
Activities: Swimming, hiking, boating, fishing, playground

Don Laine Campground   *(800) 635-0152*

790 57 Drive   *(610) 381-3381*
Palmerton, PA 18071

Season: April to October
Facilities: RV, tent, water, electricity, sewage, dump station, flush toilets, telephone, showers
Amenities: Store, snack bar, picnic tables, fire ring
Activities: Swimming, hiking, recreation hall, playground

Fern Ridge Campground

(800) 468-2442
(717) 646-2267

PO Box 707
Blakeslee, PA 18610

Season: April to October
Facilities: RV, tent, water, electricity, dump station, flush toilets, telephone, showers
Amenities: Store, picnic tables, fire ring
Activities: Swimming, fishing, recreation hall, playground

Four Seasons Campground

(717) 629-2504

RD #1, Box 18
Scotrun, PA 18355

Season: April to October
Facilities: RV, tent, water, electricity, sewage, dump station, flush toilets, telephone, showers
Amenities: Store, picnic tables, fire ring
Activities: Swimming, recreation hall, playground

Foxwood Family Campground

(800) 845-4938
(717) 421-1424

RD #8, Box 8154
Mount Nebo Drive East
Stroudsburg, PA 18301

Season: April to October
Facilities: RV, tent, water, electricity, sewage, dump station, flush toilets, telephone, showers
Amenities: Store, picnic tables, fire ring
Activities: Swimming, fishing, recreation hall, playground

Hemlock Campground

(717) 894-4388

362 Hemlock Drive
Tobyhanna, PA 18466

Season: May to October
Facilities: RV, tent, water, electricity, sewage, dump station, flush toilets, telephone, showers
Amenities: Store, picnic tables, fire ring
Activities: Swimming, recreation hall, playground

Jim Thorpe Camping Resort   (717) 325-2644

PO Box 328
Lentz Trail
Jim Thorpe, PA 18229

Season: April to October
Facilities: RV, tent, cabins, water, electricity, sewage, dump station, flush toilets, showers, telephone
Amenities: Store, picnic tables, fire ring
Activities: Swimming, hiking, fishing, recreation hall, playground

Keen Lake Camping and Cottage Resort   (800) 443-0412

RR#1, Box 1976	*(717) 488-5522*
Waymart, PA 18472	*(717) 488-6161*

Season: May to September
Facilities: RV, tent, water, electricity, sewage, dump station, flush toilets, pit toilets, telephone, showers
Amenities: Store, snack bar, picnic tables, fire ring
Activities: Swimming, hiking, boating, boat rental, fishing, recreation hall, playground

Kens Woods Campground   (717) 588-6381

RR #1, Box 506
Bushkill, PA 18324

Season: April to October
Facilities: RV, tent, water, electricity, sewage, dump station, flush toilets, telephone, showers
Amenities: Store, picnic tables, fire ring
Activities: Swimming, fishing, recreation hall, playground

Maplerock Campsite   (717) 629-0100

RR #1, Box 136
Henryville, PA 18332

Season: April to October
Facilities: RV, tent, water, electricity, sewage, dump station, flush toilets, showers
Amenities: Store, picnic tables, fire ring
Activities: Fishing, playground

Mountain Vista Campground   (717) 223-0111

RD #2, Box 2190
East Stroudsburg, PA 18301

Season: April to October
Facilities: RV, tent, water, electricity, sewage, dump station, flush toilets, telephone, showers
Amenities: Store, picnic tables, fire ring
Activities: Swimming, fishing, recreation hall, playground

Otter Lake Camp   (800) 345-1369

Box 850   (717) 223-0123
Marshalls Creek, PA 18335

Season: Year-round
Facilities: RV, tent, water, electricity, sewage, dump station, flush toilets, telephone, showers
Amenities: Store, snack bar, picnic tables, fire ring
Activities: Swimming, hiking, boating, boat rental, fishing, recreation hall, playground

Otto's Camping Resort and RV Center   (610) 377-5313

1500 Rock Street   (800) 412-4456
Lehighton, PA 18235

Season: Year-round
Facilities: RV, tent, water, electricity, sewage, dump station, flush toilets, telephone, showers
Amenities: Store, snack bar, picnic tables, fire ring
Activities: Swimming, fishing, recreation hall, playground

Pennsylvania Trivia

Jim Thorpe was formally known as Mauch Chunk. This name is from the Native American words "machk tschunk" meaning "where there is a mountain resort of bears."

PP and L Lake Wallenpaupack Camping

8428-0211
Box 122   *(717) 226-3702*
Hawley, PA
Write for brochure on all four campgrounds
   ***Caffrey**: (717) 226-4608*
   ***Ironwood Point**: (717) 857-0880*
   ***Ledgewood**: (717) 689-2181*
   ***Wilsonville**: (717) 226-4382*

Season: April to October
Facilities: RV, tent, water, electricity, dump station (Ironwood, Ledgewood, Wilsonville), telephone, showers
Amenities: Store, picnic tables
Activities: Boating, boat rental (Wilsonville), playground (Wilsonville, Ironwood)

Pocono Vacation Park

(717) 424-2587
RD #5, Box 5214
Stroudsburg, PA 18360

Season: April to October
Facilities: RV, tent, water, electricity, sewage, cable, dump station, flush toilets, telephone, showers
Amenities: Store, picnic tables, fire rings
Activities: Swimming, recreation hall, playground

River Beach Campsites

(800) FLOAT-KC
Routes 209 and 6, Box 382   *(717) 296-7421*
Milford, PA 18337

Season: March to November
Facilities: RV, tent, water, electricity, dump station, flush toilets, telephone, showers
Amenities: Store, snack bar (summer only), picnic tables, fire ring
Activities: Boating, boat rentals, fishing, recreation hall,

Tri-State Canoe and Campground *(800) 56-CANOE*

Box 400, Shay Lane *(717) 491-2173*
Matamoras, PA 18336

Season: Year-round
Facilities: RV, tent, water, electricity, sewage, dump station, flush toilets, telephone, showers
Amenities: Store, picnic tables, grills, fire ring
Activities: Swimming, boating, boat rental, fishing

WT Family Camping, Inc. *(717) 646-4040*

HC #1, Box 1486, Route 115
Blakeslee, PA 18610

Season: Year-round
Facilities: RV, tent, water, electricity, sewage, dump station, flush toilets, telephone, showers
Amenities: Store, picnic tables, fire ring
Activities: Swimming, hiking, recreation hall, playground

Pennsylvania Trivia

The state tree is the hemlock.

CHAPTER

2

ANIMALS

● ●

Animals play a large part in a child's world. Animals are the stars of many major motion pictures, they are main characters in books, and most children have slept with a stuffed one once or twice. It's no wonder that a visit to a zoo or a petting farm can generate ear-to-ear smiles. A visit to one of the spots listed below will guarantee a good time for all.

Children will love the friendly animals in a petting zoo. Photo courtesy Pocono Mountains Vacation Bureau, Inc.

Apple Tree Farm *(717) 839-7680*

Route #1, Box 9
Grange Road
Mount Pocono, PA 18344

Description: Hop a ride on the Apple Blossom Special Train, or enjoy horse-drawn wagon rides and pony rides at $3 a person. Enjoy the petting farm with lots of friendly animals. Special festivals are held throughout the year. Bakery goods and picnic facilities are available on-site.

Hours: Seven days a week, 10 a.m. to 4:30 p.m.

Cost: $4 for adults, $4 for children ages 2 to 11, and free for children under 2.

Claws and Paws Wild Animal Park *(717) 698-6154*

RD #6
Route 590
Lake Ariel, PA 18436

Description: With 120 different species including giraffes, lions, and tigers, the petting zoo and farmyard will be fun for the entire family and a great opportunity to use your camera. Educational animal shows are given from Memorial Day through Labor Day. A snack bar and picnic area are available on premises. Yearly passes are available.

Hours: May through October: seven days a week, 10 a.m. to 6 p.m.

Cost: $7.95 for adults, $4.95 for children ages 2 to 11, and free for children under 2.

Pennsylvania Trivia

The state bird is the ruffed grouse.

Pocono Snake and Animal Farm   *(717) 223-8653*

PO Box 238
Route 209
Marshalls Creek, PA 18335   ♙♙ ♿ ⚲

Description: Snakes, snakes, and more snakes plus plenty more to offer. A black bear, a tiger, exotic animals, deer, and some very entertaining monkeys. The animal exhibits change from time to time. One time you may see a baby tiger, the next you may be able to hold baby bunnies. As you enter the petting zoo, you will be greeted by some native white-tail deer.

Hours: March through June and September through November: Monday through Friday, 11 a.m. to 5 p.m.; Saturday and Sunday, 11 a.m. to 7 p.m. July and August: daily, 11 a.m. to 7 p.m. Closed on rainy days.

Cost: $3.50 for adults, $2.50 for children ages 2 to 12, and free for children under 2.

"Don't be afraid, he won't bite." Get a close view of some of the world's snakes and many other animals at the Pocono Snake and Animal Farm.
Photo courtesy Pocono Mountains Vacation Bureau, Inc.

On your visit to Quiet Valley Living Historical Farm, discover what children used to do for fun in the 18th Century. Photo courtesy Pocono Mountains Vacation Bureau, Inc.

Quiet Valley Living Historical Farm   *(717) 992-6161*

1000 Turkey Hill Road
Stroudsburg, PA 18360

Description: This quaint setting of an original Pennsylvania Dutch farm is home to many farm animals. Tours are given by role players that interpret the story of 18th-century farm life. Three festivals are held during the year: Farm Animal Frolic in May; Harvest Festival in October; and Old Time Christmas in December. Memberships are available.

Hours: June 20th to Labor Day and special times during the year: Monday through Saturday, 9:30 a.m. to 5:30 p.m.; Sunday, 1 p.m. to 5:30 p.m. The last tour begins at 4 p.m. Call for further information.

Cost: $6 for adults, $3.50 for children ages 3 to 12, and free for children under 3.

Reptiland
(717) 538-1869

RD #1, Box 388
Route 15
Allenwood, PA 17810

Description: In addition to reptiles, you will see 30 different species of exotic birds. During the summer months there are five animal shows daily: 10:30 a.m., 12 noon, 1:30 p.m., 3 p.m., and 4:30 p.m. A snack bar and picnic tables are on the premises. Memberships are available.

Hours: July through August: daily, 9 a.m. to 7 p.m. April, May, September, and October: daily, 10 a.m. to 6 p.m. November through March: daily, 10 a.m. to 5 p.m.

Cost: $7 for adults, $5 for children ages 4 to 11, and free for children under 4.

Trexler-Lehigh County Game Preserve
(610) 799-4171

5150 Game Preserve Road
Schnecksville, PA 18078

Description: More than just a zoo, the Trexler-Lehigh County Game Preserve offers over 1500 acres to discover wild animals. The game preserve was established not only to entertain, but to educate. Daily activity schedules will keep you hopping from one event to another. An outdoor cafe and picnic area are available, as well as pony rides, and nature trails for hiking. The petting zoo enables your children to come face to face with tame and baby animals. Plan to spend the day.

Hours: Memorial Day through Labor Day: daily, 10 a.m. to 4:30 p.m. April, May, September, and October: Saturday and Sunday only, 10 a.m. to 4:30 p.m.

Cost: $5 for adults, $3 for senior citizens, and $3 for children ages 2 to 12.

Pennsylvania Trivia

The state animal is the whitetail deer.

Visitors to the House of Candles will get a chance to watch the art of candle making. Photo courtesy Pocono Mountains Vacation Bureau, Inc.

CHAPTER
3

DEMONSTRATIONS

• •

Young and old alike enjoy seeing how things are made. Take a ride to one of the places listed below for an educational demonstration of candy, pretzel, candle, or pottery making

Callie's Candy Kitchen   *(717) 595-2280*

PO Box 126
Route 390   *www.calliescandy.com*
Mountainhome, PA 18342   ⊗ ♥♥ ё ♪

Description: The candy maker gives a demonstration about how candy is made. The format is informal and questions from the audience are encouraged. During the demonstration samples are passed around. Tour seekers must call first to schedule a tour or see if one is being planned. The candy shop is incredible.

Hours: Year-round except January: daily, 10 a.m. to 5 p.m.
Cost: Free.

Pennsylvania Trivia

The state nickname is the Keystone State.

Callie's Pretzel Factory *(717) 595-3257*

PO Box 395
Routes 390 and 191 *www.calliescandy.com*
Cresco, PA 18326

Description: At this old house converted into a pretzel factory, your group will be able to view the product being made through the safety of glass and get a tasty treat in the gift shop. You're also in for a surprise if you are left handed. This shop offers a left-handed section with gifts for the southpaws in your life.

Hours: June through December: daily, 10 a.m. to 5 p.m. January through March: Saturday and Sunday, 10 a.m. to 5 p.m. Call for the April and May hours.

Cost: Free.

Holley Ross Pottery Factory and Showroom *(717) 676-3248*

RD #2
Route 191
Cresco, PA 18326

Description: This place is more than just a pottery shop. In addition to pottery demonstrations, a swinging bridge and hiking trails are located next to the factory. Groups must call to schedule.

Hours: May through mid-December: Monday through Friday, demonstrations are scheduled at 11 a.m. and 3:30 p.m.

Cost: Free.

Pennsylvania Trivia

The design for Disney World's Haunted Mansion was inspired by the Harry Packer Mansion located next to the Asa Packer Mansion in Jim Thorpe.

House of Candles

(717) 629-1953

PO Box 530
Route 715 North
Henryville, PA 18332

Description: This family-owned and operated candle shop is the oldest in the area. The shop offers visitors a chance to see candles carved. As an added attraction, there are also some animals outside for the young ones to view. It is recommended that groups call to ensure that the candle maker can be there when your group arrives.

Hours: Year-round: Monday through Saturday, 10 a.m. to 5 p.m.
Cost: Free.

Pennsylvania Trivia

Knock, Knock.
Who's there?.
Pencil.
Pencil Who?
Pennsylvania, that's who!

The quaint town of Jim Thorpe is full of history. Photo courtesy Pocono Mountains Vacation Bureau, Inc.

CHAPTER

4

HISTORY

• •

The variety of historical attractions in the Poconos offers a look at the role the region played in shaping the history of America. The area is rich with the history of Native Americans and early colonists, the industrial revolution, and the bygone mining industry. Visiting one of these sites with a child can be especially meaningful. A child's imagination and fresh point of view will make trips to the historic sites much more interesting. When children are able to actually touch a real arrowhead or sit in a one-room schoolhouse, they can truly appreciate not only the past but the present.

If you are planning to take a school group to one of the sites listed, please call in advance and make appropriate arrangements. Inquire about group rates and picnic facilities. You will find that all the staff members are eager to share their knowledge of the past with young minds.

Antoine Dutot School and Museum   *(717) 476-0365*

PO Box 484
Main Street
Delaware Water Gap, PA 18327   ♥♥♥ ⟨

Description: A brick schoolhouse displays a photo history of the Delaware Water Gap as a vacation spot. An accompanying slide show describes this story in greater detail. Artwork from local artists is displayed on the surrounding walls and changes periodically. Memberships are available.

Hours: Memorial Day through October: Saturday and Sunday, 1 p.m. to 5 p.m.

Cost: $1 for adults and $.50 for children.

Asa Packer Mansion   *(717) 325-3229*

c/o Carbon County Office
Pocono Mountain Vacation Bureau
PO Box 27
Jim Thorpe, PA 18229   ♀♂ ᕷ ⟨

Description: The 1861 residence of Asa Packer is in its original state, left exactly as it was when the Packers lived there. Asa Packer, the founder of Lehigh University in Bethlehem, Pennsylvania, was involved in railroads and politics. The tour of the mansion offers plenty of local history. Group tours may be made by appointment.

Hours: Memorial Day through October: daily, 11 a.m. to 4:15 p.m. April and May: weekends only, 11 a.m. to 4:15 p.m.

Cost: $5 for adults, $3 for children ages 12 and under.

Burnside Plantation, Inc.   *(610) 868-5044*

PO Box 1305   *School Tours: (610) 691-0603*
1461 Schoenersville Road
Bethlehem, PA 18017   ⬛ ⊛ ♀♂ ⟨

Description: As one of the members of the Historic Bethlehem Partnership, the Burnside Plantation is a 6½-acre tract of land that is home to an original 1749 Moravian farmhouse complete with summer kitchen, barn and shed, wagon shed, corn crib, and apple orchard. A visit here offers a look at the Moravian agricultural history. The farm is available for self-guided tours, but is also a popular school group destination. Festivals and fun family days, demonstrations, workshops, and children's programs are scheduled throughout the year. The plantation also offers a sampling of special group programs including "Colonial Time Travelers" and a summer history camp.

Hours: Monday through Friday, 8:30 a.m. to 5 p.m. Weekend tours by appointment. Self-guided tours are always available when the grounds are open.

Cost: $3 for non-members, $2 for members.

Bushkill Falls   *(717) 588-6682*

Bushkill Falls Road
Bushkill, PA 18324

Description: Enjoy some of the natural history of the Poconos. Billed as the "Niagara of Pennsylvania," Bushkill Falls lives up to its reputation as you hike for two hours on four trails where you will discover eight waterfalls in a pristine natural setting. After the hike, enjoy the Native American museum which depicts the life of the Lenni-Lenapes, a tribe native to the Pocono region. The museum also has a wildlife exhibit displaying the animals that inhabit the Poconos and the Pennsylvania region. Miniature golf, paddleboats, picnic areas, shops, and a fudge kitchen make the day complete.

Hours: April through November: Monday through Friday, 9 a.m. to 5 p.m.; Saturday and Sunday, 9 a.m. to 6 p.m. Memorial Day through Labor Day: daily, 9 a.m. to 6 p.m.

Cost: $7 for adults, $6.25 for senior citizens, $2 for children ages 4 to 10, and free for children under 4.

Columns Museum   *(717) 296-8126*

PO Box 915
Milford, PA 18337

Description: This museum houses a collection of early American and local history displays, including Native American artifacts, an original Mayflower candlestick, the Lincoln flag, a vintage costume collection, and so much more for you to see. Memberships to the museum are available.

Hours: April through December: Wednesday, Saturday, and Sunday, 1 p.m. to 4 p.m.

Cost: $2 for adults, $.50 for children ages 12 and under.

Driebe Freight Station   *(717) 424-1776*

537 Ann Street
Stroudsburg, PA 18360    *(1st floor only)*

Description: An old train station is host to a country store, train artifacts, a blacksmith shop, and other displays that rotate throughout the year. The museum is administered by the Monroe County Historical Association and sponsors children's workshops throughout the year, which give the participants a firsthand appreciation for the crafts of yesteryear.

Hours: Year-round: Wednesday through Saturday, 12 noon to 4 p.m.

Cost: $2 is the suggested donation for adults, $1 for children.

Eckley Miner's Village   *(717) 636-2070*

RR #2, Box 236
Weatherly, PA 18255
Location: Eckley, PA

Description: A village dating back to 1854 depicts the life of a family in a mining village. A museum on the premises offers an orientation film and exhibits of how a miner's family lived. Other buildings include the doctor's office, two churches, and a double mining home showing both how miners lived in the early days and how their living quarters changed over time. Group tours are available year-round by appointment. The walking tour takes two to three hours.

Hours: Memorial Day through Labor Day: Monday through Saturday, 9 a.m. to 5 p.m.; Sunday, 12 noon to 5 p.m.

Cost: $3.50 for adults, $3 for senior citizens; $1.50 for children ages 6 to 12, free for children 5 and under. Family Rate $8.50 (with an additional $1 per adult and $.50 per child).

Grey Towers National Historic Landmark   *(717) 296-9630*

U.S. Forest Service
PO Box 188
Milford, PA 18837

Description: Grey Towers shows how it was to live in Victorian times. The 41-room mansion was once the home of former Pennsylvania governor Gifford Pinchot. If you visit during the spring and summer months, take a walk around the grounds after you finish touring the interior and enjoy the beautiful walkways and gardens.

Hours: Year-round: Friday through Monday, 10 a.m. to 4 p.m. Tours every hour.

Cost: Donations are suggested.

Grey Towers National Historic Landmark is beautiful both inside and out. Photo courtesy Pocono Mountains Vacation Bureau, Inc.

Houdini Tour and Magic Show — *(717) 342-5555*

1433 North Main Avenue   www.microserve.net/magicusa/hoidini.html
Scranton, PA 18508   e-mail: magicusa@microserve.net

Description: For those families who are intrigued with magic and the art of escape, you will want to experience this two-hour tour and magic show. Begin with an orientation video and finish with a magic show, which features lots of fun and laughs. You will see actual artifacts from the Houdini collection. Tours are continuous throughout the day.

Hours: Memorial Day to Labor Day: daily, 11 a.m. to 6 p.m. except for the first two weeks of June when the hours are 1 p.m. to 5 p.m.

Cost: $7.50 for adults, $6 for children ages 11 and under.

Liberty Bell Shrine — *(610) 435-4232*

Zion's Reformed Church
620 Hamilton Street
Allentown, PA 18101

Description: The Zion's Reformed Church is where the Liberty Bell was hidden during the American Revolution. It is said that after the Battle of Brandywine in 1777, George Washington had lost hope of saving Philadelphia from the British. The Liberty Bell was, therefore, secretly moved by wagon to this church for safekeeping. A mural and audio tape tell the story. Tour guides are available. Large groups need to make appointments for tours.

Hours: Monday through Saturday, 12 noon to 4 p.m. Closed on major holidays.

Cost: A donation is requested.

Mauch Chunk Museum — *(717) 325-9190*

40 West Broadway
Jim Thorpe, PA 18229

Description: This museum tells the story of Mauch Chunk from the discovery of coal to present. Mauch Chunk, now known as Jim Thorpe, claims to be responsible for the start of the industrial revolution. Museum membership benefits are available.

Hours: May through October: Thursday through Saturday, 10 a.m. to 5 p.m.; Sunday, 12 noon to 5 p.m. During the school year call for a private tour.

Cost: $2 is the suggested donation for adults, $1 for children.

National Canal Museum *(610) 515-8000*

Two Rivers Landing
30 Centre Square   *www.crayola.com*
Easton, PA 18042-7744

Description: The National Canal Museum, which shares a roof with the Crayola Factory (*see* Chapter 13), is housed in the top floor, and brings back to life the canal system on the Lehigh and Delaware Rivers. Start with an orientation video and proceed to view the museum which houses replicas of an actual canal boat and other artifacts. This tour should be coupled with the Crayola Factory and would make a great rainy day activity. However, the capacity of the building is limited and strictly enforced. It is highly recommended that you make arrangements for a visit to avoid disappointment. Admission price includes both the Crayola Factory and the Canal Museum. There is also a McDonald's Express on-site.

Hours: Year-round: Tuesday through Saturday, 9:30 a.m. to 5 p.m.; Sunday, 12 noon to 5 p.m. Closed most Mondays and all major holidays.

Cost: $6 for adults and children, $5.50 for senior citizens, and free for children under 2.

Old Jail *(717) 325-5259*

128 Broadway
Jim Thorpe, PA 18229

Description: When the village of Jim Thorpe was monopolized by the mine owners, the Molly Maguires (an underground labor organization) tried to improve the conditions of the miners and the mining families. These rebels pleaded their cause with ruthless and intimidating methods. One of the Molly Maguires arrested claimed his innocence before he was hung. Placing his hand on the wall of Cell 17, he stated a handprint would remain to prove this injustice. You and your detectives will have to check this one out for yourselves. Great for older children.

Hours: May through October: Thursday through Tuesday, 12 noon to 4:30 p.m.
Cost: $4 for adults, $3.50 for senior citizens, $2.50 for children ages 6 to 12, and free for children under 6.

Pennsylvania Anthracite Heritage Museum
(717) 963-4804

RD #1, Bald Mountain Road
Scranton, PA 18504 ♦♦♦ ♿ ♫

Description: This museum depicts the life of the miner, his family, and the culture created by the coal industry. Take about a 45-minute walk through a pictorial history of the national coal and textile industry, and enjoy this culturally and historically enriching experience. This is a great activity to couple with the Lackawanna Coal Mine Tour (*see* Chapter 13).
Hours: April through October: Tuesday through Saturday, 9 a.m. to 5 p.m.; Sunday, 12 noon to 5 p.m. Open Independence Day, Labor Day, and Memorial Day.
Cost: $3.50 for adults, $3 for senior citizens, $2 for children ages 6 to 12, and free for children 5 and under. Family tickets are available for $12.

Pocono Indian Museum
(717) 588-9338

PO Box 261
Route 209
Bushkill, PA 18324

www.gmcreations.com/IndianMuseum
e-mail: dream38@postoffice.ptd.net.
♦♦♦ ♿ ♫

Description: The history of the Delaware Indians is re-created for a self-guided tour. With an audio tape as your tour guide you will be able to view the museum at your own pace. Groups of 20 or more will be accompanied by a guide. During your tour, you will see arrowheads, a peace pipe, ornate beadwork, and other artifacts. You will get a feel of what life on the Delaware was like. The attached gift shop is as interesting as the museum.
Hours: June through August: Sunday through Thursday, 9 a.m. to 7 p.m.; Friday and Saturday, 9 a.m. to 8 p.m. September through May: Monday through Friday, 10 a.m. to 6 p.m.; Saturday and Sunday, 9:30 a.m. to 7 p.m.
Cost: $3.50 for adults, $2.50 for senior citizens, $2 for children ages 6 to 16, and free for children under 6.

Quiet Valley Living Historical Farm   *(717) 992-6161*

PO Box 696
1000 Turkey Hill Road
Stroudsburg, PA 18360

Description: Costumed guides share a day on the farm as it would
be from the mid-1700s through the early 1900s. The guides role-
play to help the guests relive history. This farm is particularly
exciting for school group tours. Quiet Valley offers groups a step
back into a one-room schoolhouse during this 3½-hour experience. Farm Hands Adventure gives children a chance to churn
butter, grind flour, and assist with other chores that life on the
farm had to offer. Quiet Valley will also travel to classrooms to
tell an old-time story, bringing a special farmyard animal to assist. Workshops are offered throughout the year. Call to get the
most current information. Festivals are hosted at the farm sea-
sonally throughout the year (*see* Chapter 5), allowing children
to participate in games and activities that were typical for youth
in the 18th and 19th centuries. A picnic grove is available.

Hours: June 20th through Labor Day: Tuesday through Saturday, 10
a.m. to 5:30 p.m.; Sunday, 1 p.m. to 5:30 p.m. The last tour begins at 4 p.m. Also open for special times during the year. Call
for further information on birthday parties and off-season hours.

Cost: $6 for adults, $3.50 for children ages 3 to 12, free for children
under 3.

Scranton Iron Furnaces   *(717) 963-3208*

159 Cedar Avenue
Scranton, PA 18505

Description: The Scranton Iron Furnaces are four stone-blast fur-
nace stacks built in the mid-1800s. The facility was the second
largest iron producer in the United States by the 1880s. The mill
produced T rails for America's railroads up until 1902. The site
is in walking distance of the Steamtown National Historical site
in Scranton. Take a guided or self-guided tour to learn how iron
ore was made and used to make railroad tracks. Guided tours
need to be scheduled prior to visiting.

Hours: April through October: Tuesday through Sunday, 9 a.m. to 5
p.m. Closed Monday. Open on Independence Day, Memorial
Day, and Labor Day. Call for hours November through March.

Cost: $3 for adults and children.

Soldiers and Sailors Monument

Centre Square
Easton, PA 18042

Description: The Soldiers and Sailors Monument, located in Centre Square, is the site of Northampton County's first courthouse, built in 1765 on a tract presented by the Penn family. The annual rent was one red rose. The first reading of the Declaration of Independence to the Colonists took place on the steps of this courthouse. It is situated directly across the street from the Crayola Factory (*see* Chapter 13) and the Canal Museum in this chapter.
Hours: Year-round: daily, dawn to dusk.
Cost: Free.

Stroud Mansion   *(717) 421-7703*

900 Main Street
Stroudsburg, PA 18360

Description: This home was built by Jacob Stroud, founder of Stroudsburg, for one of his children. Exhibits include Stroud family artifacts, antique toys, and memorabilia from the Revolutionary War, the Civil War, and both World Wars.
Hours: Year-round: Tuesday through Friday, 10 a.m. to 4 p.m.; Sunday, 1 p.m. to 4 p.m.
Cost: $2 is the suggested donation for adults, $1 for senior citizens and children.

Wayne County Historical Society Museum   *(717) 253-3240*

PO Box 446
810 Main Street
Honesdale, PA 18431

Description: This museum is home a replica of the Stourbridge Lion, the first locomotive to run on a commercial track in America. The Faces in Clay exhibit portrays the life and history of Native Americans from the Upper Delaware River Valley. A glass exhibit displays works from some of the glass shops that once occupied Wayne County. Guided tours need to be arranged in advance.
Hours: Call for current times because the hours change every season.
Cost: $3 for adults, $2 for children ages 12 to 18, free for children under 12.

Zane Grey Museum

(717) 685-4871

RD #2, Box 2428
Beach Lake, PA 18405-9737
Physical location: Lackawaxen, PA

www.nps.gov/upde
e-mail: from web site
👨‍👩‍👦 🐾

Description: The home of novelist Zane Grey is open to the public for tours. Zane Grey, author of the popular *Riders of the Purple Sage*, was noted for writing novels about the Wild West. His research and writing rooms are open, displaying personal memorabilia. In addition to his fame as an author, Grey was known for his skill as a fisherman and outdoorsman. Any young cowpoke would enjoy this ranch.

Hours: Varies based on funding. Call for details.

Cost: Free.

Historical Societies

For more information about children's programs close to you, contact the historical society in your area.

Mauch Chunk Historical Society

(717) 325-4439

14 West Broadway
Jim Thorpe, PA 18229

Monroe County Historical Society

(717) 424-1776

900 Main Street
Stroudsburg, PA 18360

Pike County Historical Society

(717) 296-8126

PO Box 915
Milford, PA 18337

Wayne County Historical Society

(717) 253-3240

PO Box 446
810 Main Street
Honesdale, PA, 18431

Enjoy a step back into history at Quiet Valley Historical Farm. Photo courtesy Pocono Mountains Vacation Bureau, Inc.

CHAPTER

5

FESTIVALS AND CELEBRATIONS

• •

As all parents know, children make any celebration all the more special. Just think how much fun your child will have when the special event is geared toward kids. The events listed here include a selection of well established celebrations and festivals in the Poconos. Keep your eyes open for new ones and send them in for consideration in the next edition.

January

Pennsylvania Learn to Ski Free Day   *(800) 762-6667*

A special day honored at all the area ski slopes for your family to learn to ski at a reduced price. Call one of the ski areas in Chapter 12 to get details for that particular resort.

March

Maple Sugaring   *(717) 629-3061*

Sponsored annually by the Monroe County Environmental Education Center, this event is a great time for the entire family. Staff members hike into the woods with your group and tap a tree to demonstrate how maple syrup is harvested. The event concludes with a pancake and syrup treat on the trail.

St. Patrick's Day Parade   *(717) 476-6568*

c/o Pocono Irish American Club
Main Street
Stroudsburg, PA

Don your kilt and come join the 30,000 plus spectators lining the main streets of Stroudsburg and East Stroudsburg, and listen to the many professional pipe and drum bands and drum and bugle corps. You don't have to be Irish to feel lucky at this parade. The annual parade is held the Sunday after St. Patrick's Day.

April

Bunny Run   *(717) 253-1960*

Stourbridge Line
Honesdale, PA

Easter Bunny Trail Rides   *(717) 325-3673*

Rail Tours: Train Depot
Jim Thorpe, PA

These two train rides band the excitement of the ride with a visit from the Easter Bunny. What a great way to welcome this spring holiday.

Healthy Kids Day   *(717) 421-2525*

Pocono YMCA
809 Main Street
Stroudsburg, PA 18360

The Pocono YMCA opens its doors to children and adults alike on Healthy Kids Day. The day is filled with crafts, games, open swim, a preschool tumbling area, demonstrations, safety presentations, and lots of other fun and educational things that kids love. While you are there, take a look at the many programs available at the YMCA for your family.

Pennsylvania Trivia

The state insect is the firefly.

May

Farm Animal Frolic   (717) 992-6161

Quiet Valley Living Historical Farm
1000 Turkey Hill Road
Stroudsburg, PA 18360

Come witness all the new life blossoming every spring at Quiet Valley. The farm is alive with baby animals, demonstrations, and fabulous food.

Laurel Blossom Festival   (717) 325-3673

Asa Packer Park
Jim Thorpe, PA

Enjoy the charming town of Jim Thorpe when it's enhanced by crafters and food vendors. Train rides, as well as many other attractions in the town, will make for a relaxing family day.

Laurel Festival of the Arts   (717) 325-3441

Mauch Chunk National Historic District
Jim Thorpe, PA

A two-week concert series sponsored by the Mauch Chunk Historical Society presents a variety of classical music. In addition to the main concerts, there are special art exhibits, poetry readings, and children's programs. Call for rates and a schedule of events.

June

Cranberry Bog Nature Walk   (717) 629-3061

Monroe County Environmental Education Center
8050 Running Valley Road
Stroudsburg, PA 18360

This nature walk through the bog explores the environment of the area in the summertime.

Free Fishing Day in Pennsylvania   *(717) 477-5717*

Pennsylvania Fish Commission
Northeast Region

Every year in June the Pennsylvania Fish Commission sponsors a free day of fishing in June. This day allows anglers to fish in Pennsylvania legally without purchasing a license. Call the Northeast Regional office of the Pennsylvania Fish Commission to inquire about the date.

Kid Fest   *(717) 421-7231*

Shawnee Place
Shawnee on Delaware, PA 18356

This festival was planned with kids in mind. This weekend is filled with entertainment from storytellers and magicians, with plenty of music and kid fun.

Mountain Bike Weekend   *(717) 325-3669*

Mauch Chunk Lake Park
Jim Thorpe, PA

Clinics and organized bike rides make this event the largest noncompetitive mountain biking event in the eastern United States. The many trails that surround the Jim Thorpe area add to the enjoyment of the weekend.

Strawberry Festivals

Strawberry festivals usher in summer in the Poconos. In the peak of strawberry-picking season, many area churches and organizations offer food festivals with scrumptious strawberry selections. Look in the local newspaper for dates and locations.

July

Fireworks

Many area resorts host firework displays. Check the local newspaper for dates and locations.

August

Bethlehem Musikfest   (610) 861-0678

22 Bethlehem Plaza
Bethlehem, PA 18018

This annual musical extravaganza starts the second Saturday in August and keeps Bethlehem swinging for nine days. During that time, over 300 musical groups, ranging from blues to Bach to bebop, perform over 650 concerts on 17 different stages. There are many street performers for the young to enjoy and lots of food. The best part is that most of the entertainment is free!

Fairs

Green-Dreher Sterling Fair   (717) 646-4047
Newfoundland, PA

Wayne County Fair   (717) 253-1108
Honesdale, PA

West End Fair   (610) 381-3199
West End Fairgrounds   (610) 681-4293

Just what you would expect a country fair to be. These fairs attract people from across northeastern Pennsylvania with first-rate entertainment, fantastic foods, farm animals, agricultural shows and displays, carnival rides, and special events for the whole family to enjoy.

September

Celebration of the Arts   (717) 424-2210

Delaware Water Gap, PA

This outdoor arts festival consumes the charming town of Delaware Water Gap with jazz musicians, artists, and scrumptious food. A great way to enjoy the end of summer.

Pike County Family Fair   (717) 296-8700

Airport Park   (717) 296-8790
Milford, PA

Renowned for the watermelon seed spitting contest, this local fair promises to please everyone.

October

Autumn Balloon Festival   *(717) 421-1500*

Shawnee Inn and Golf Resort
Shawnee on the Delaware, PA

If hot air balloons are your thing, then this is the festival for you. In addition to the many balloons being launched, there is lots of entertainment specifically for children including a puppet show, clowns, carnival rides, and more.

Fall Foliage Festival   *(717) 325-3673*

Asa Packer Park
Jim Thorpe, PA

Special events, food vendors, and crafters make this a wonderful autumn frolic.

The Autumn Ballon Festival hosted by Shawnee Inn is a popular and fun event. Photo courtesy Pocono Mountains Vacation Bureau, Inc.

Harvest Festival
(717) 992-6161

Quiet Valley Living Historical Farm
1000 Turkey Hill Road
Stroudsburg, PA 18360

Volunteers from Quiet Valley dress in period costume and spend the weekend acting out the typical tasks and daily routines of early Pennsylvania Dutch farm life. Numerous demonstrations are performed and interaction is welcome. Families can sample homemade bread, griddle cakes, and ice cream. There are also old-fashioned games for all to enjoy and pony rides for the kids.

Halloween and Autumn Festivals

The events listed below offer lots of fall fun for everyone. Pumpkin picking, haunted hayrides, corn mazes, and fresh-squeezed cider are welcome signs of autumn. Call any one of these locations for further details.

Annual Barrett Township Halloween Parade
(717) 595-7752

RD #1, Box 155
Scarecrowville Station
Canadensis, PA 18325

The Great Pocono Pumpkin Patch Festival
(610) 377-5050

Country Junction, Route 209
Forest Inn, PA

Halloween Extravaganza and Parade
(717) 424-9131

Main Street
Stroudsburg, PA

Haunted Hayrides
(717) 226-2620

Triple W Riding Stable
Honesdale, PA

Hawley Harvest Hoe-down

(717) 226-3191

Hawley, PA

Pumpkin Patch and Homecoming Festival

(610) 381-3582

Old Homestead Tree Farm
Kunkletown, PA

December

Christmas of Olde

(610) 377-5050

Country Junction, Route 209
Route 209
Forest Inn, PA

Christmas Village

(717) 424-1776

The Stroudsburg Fire Department Christmas Village
Located next to the Driebe Freight Station
537 Ann Street
Stroudsburg, PA 18360

In a Stroudsburg tradition, Santa and Rudolph host this miniature Christmas Village.

Old Time Christmas

(717) 992-6161

Quiet Valley Living Historical Farm
1000 Turkey Hill Road
Stroudsburg, PA 18360

Tours of the 18th-century farm are offered on weekends in December. Costumed guides take you through the farm and discuss how Christmas was celebrated in the past. A live barnyard nativity scene is part of the tour.

Olde Time Christmas Celebration   *(717) 325-3673*

Jim Thorpe, PA

The arrival of Santa sparks the beginning of this annual celebration. Tree trimming, children's theater productions, caroling, and Christmas concerts amidst the yuletide decorations of this quaint town add to the magic of this special season.

Santa Claus Train Rides   *(717) 325-3675*

Rail Tours, Inc.
Jim Thorpe, PA

Ride the train with Santa along the Lehigh River.

Santa Express   *(717) 253-1960*

Stourbridge Line Rail Excursion
742 Main Street
Honesdale, PA

Enjoy a one and a half hour holiday train trip in the company of Santa and Mrs. Claus on weekends in December.

Yuletide Celebrations   *(610) 868-1513*

Bethlehem Visitors Center
509 Main Street
Bethlehem, PA 18018

What better place to visit at Christmas than Bethlehem? A large lighted Star of Bethlehem, which can be seen for miles, is placed on the south mountain. Hundreds of lighted trees decorate the city. There is a live Christmas pageant, Moravian Christmas manger, and nightly guided bus tours with costumed guides. Call the Visitors Center for a schedule of activities.

Pennsylvania Trivia

If you would like to send a "spooktacular" Halloween greeting to friends and relatives, package up your greetings and mail them to: Postmaster, Scarecrowville Station, Canadensis, PA 18325. Your letters will be sent with a special Halloween postmark.

Storybook characters come to life at the library. Photo by Maria Horn.

CHAPTER

6

LIBRARIES

• •

Libraries are wonderful places to take your children to explore, learn, and grow. They can also be places where a child can experience firsthand that reading is fun. You could spend part of your day looking at books and reading at the story table. You may even be able to surf the Net. Most libraries are on-line and offer public access. If you are a full-time or part-time resident of the community, the library will be able to give a library card to both you and your child. A library card will enable you to check out books, magazines, videos, CDs, and at some libraries, interactive software. Inquire about PA Access at your local library. If you become a PA Access cardholder, material from other PA Access libraries are available to you on interlibrary loan. Most libraries offer special children's programs, theme days, movies, and craft time. Call ahead to see if registration is required for the programs that interest you. The listings below will help you and your child discover the library nearest you.

Carbon County

Dimmick Memorial Public Library   *(717) 325-2131*

54 Broadway
Jim Thorpe, PA 18229   ⊗ ċ ☏

Hours: Monday through Friday, 9 a.m. to 5 p.m. and 7 p.m. to 8:30 p.m.; Saturday, 9 a.m. to 12 noon. Closed Sundays.
Programs: Preschool story hour, summer reading program, Christmas story hour.

Lehighton Memorial Public Library   *(610) 377-2750*

124 North Street
Lehighton, PA 18235   ⑱ ⑤ ⑨

Hours: Monday, Wednesday, and Friday, 10 a.m. to 4:50 p.m.; Tuesday and Thursday, 1:30 p.m. to 7:50 p.m.; Saturday, 9 a.m. to 11 a.m. Closed Sundays.
Programs: Preschool story hour, summer reading program.

Palmerton Library   *(610) 826-3424*

402 Delaware Avenue
Palmerton, PA 18071   ⑱ ⑤ ⑨

Hours: September through May: Monday through Friday, 10 a.m. to 5 p.m.; Monday through Wednesday, 7 p.m. to 9 p.m.; Saturday, 10 a.m. to 12 noon. Closed Sunday.
Programs: Summer reading program, chess program, preschool story hour.

Monroe County

Barrett Friendly Library   *(717) 595-7171*

PO Box 604   *e-mail: brfpublib@hslc.org*
Route 191
Mountainhome, PA 18342   ⑱ ⑤ ⑨

Hours: Monday through Thursday, 12 noon to 5 p.m. and 6:30 p.m. to 9 p.m.; Friday, 12 noon to 4 p.m.; Saturday, 11:30 a.m. to 3 p.m. Closed Sunday.
Programs: Preschool story hour.

Clymer Library   *(717) 646-0826*

PO Box 730
Firehouse Road, Old Route 940
Pocono Pines, PA 18350   ⑱ ⑤ ⑨

Hours: Monday, Wednesday, and Friday, 10 a.m. to 5 p.m.; Tuesday and Thursday, 1 p.m. to 8 p.m.; Saturday, 10 a.m. to 2 p.m. Closed Sunday.
Programs: Preschool story hour, holiday story hours.

Eastern Monroe Public Library   *(717) 421-0800*

1002 North Ninth Street   *e-mail: monroepl@epix.net*
Stroudsburg, PA 18360   ⊗ ᕫ ⟅

Hours: Monday through Thursday, 9 a.m. to 9 p.m.; Friday, 9 a.m. to
6 p.m.; Saturday, 9 a.m. to 5 p.m. Closed Sunday.
Programs: Preschool story hour, summer reading program, summer story hour, craft club.

Kemp Library at East Stroudsburg
University   *(717) 422-3465*

200 Prospect Street   *(717) 422-3126*
East Stroudsburg, PA 18301   ⊗ ᕫ ⟅

Hours: Sunday, 2 p.m. to 10 p.m.; Monday through Friday, 8 a.m. to
11 p.m.; Saturday, 9 a.m. to 4 p.m. In the summer, the library is
closed Sunday and the hours vary.
Programs: Although you must be a student or on the staff of the
university to check out books, it is worthwhile to come here
and explore. It is a great place to research a term paper. A
children's book section is available as well.

Pocono Mountain Public Library   *(717) 894-8860*

5540 Memorial Blvd.   *e-mail: pompublib@hslc.org*
Tobyhanna, PA 18466   ⊗ ᕫ ⟅

Hours: Monday, Wednesday, Thursday, 10 a.m. to 8 p.m.; Tuesday
and Friday, 10 a.m. to 5 p.m.; Saturday, 10 a.m. to 4 p.m. Closed
Sunday.
Programs: Preschool story hour, poetry and writer's club, music
program, puppet shows.

Pocono Township Branch Library   *(717) 629-5858*

c/o Eastern Monroe Public Library
1002 North Ninth Street
Stroudsburg, PA 18360   ⊗ ᕫ ⟅
Location: Route 611, Pocono Township. Building, Tannersville

Hours: Monday, 9 a.m. to 6 p.m.; Tuesday and Wednesday, 3 p.m. to
7 p.m.; Thursday, 9 a.m. to 2 p.m.; Friday, 2 p.m. to 6 p.m.; Saturday, 10 a.m. to 2 p.m. Closed Sunday.
Programs: Preschool story hour, summer reading program.

Smithfield Branch Library
(717) 223-1881

Route 209 at Foxmoor Village
Marshalls Creek, PA 18335
⑧ ⓖ ⟡

Hours: Monday, Friday, Saturday, 10 a.m. to 2 p.m.; Tuesday and Thursday, 2 p.m. to 6 p.m. Closed Wednesday and Sunday.
Programs: Preschool story hour, craft club.

Western Pocono Community Library
(717) 992-7934

PO Box 318
Route 209 and Bond Lane
Brodheadville, PA 18321
⑧ ⓖ ⟡

Hours: Monday, 12 noon to 8 p.m.; Tuesday and Wednesday, 10 a.m. to 5 p.m.; Thursday, 10 a.m. to 8 p.m.; Friday, 10 a.m. to 3 p.m.; Saturday, 10 a.m. to 2 p.m. Closed Sunday.
Programs: Preschool story hour.

Pike County

Delaware Township Library Association
(717) 828-2226

RR#2, Box 361
Dingmans Ferry, PA 18328
⑧ ⟡

Hours: Monday and Wednesday, 1 p.m. to 4 p.m.; Saturday, 11 a.m. to 1 p.m. Closed Sunday.
Programs: Call for program information.

Dingman/Delaware Branch Library
(717) 296-3130

c/o Pike County Public Library
201 Broad Street
Milford, PA 18337
⑧ ⓖ ⟡
(Located at the Dingman/Delaware Elementary School; first door on the right)

Hours: September through June: Monday through Thursday, 4 p.m. to 8 p.m. June through August: Monday through Thursday, 9 a.m. to 1 p.m. Closed during school vacations. Closed Friday through Sunday year-round.
Programs: Summer reading program.

Greeley Branch Library

(717) 685-3100

St. Luke's Center
PO Box 45
Route 590   *e-mail: grepubli@pikeonline.net*
Greeley, PA 18425   ⊗ ⧏ ⚲

Hours: Monday, 2 p.m. to 7 p.m.; Tuesday, Wednesday, and Saturday, 12 noon to 5 p.m.; Thursday, 10 a.m. to 3 p.m. Closed Friday and Sunday.
Programs: Summer reading program, preschool story hour.

Pike County Public Library

(717) 296-8211

201 Broad Street   *e-mail: pikpubli@warwick.net*
Milford, PA 18337   *members.tripod.com/pikepubliclibrary/index.html*
⊗ ⧏ ⚲

Hours: Monday and Tuesday, 10 a.m. to 9 p.m.; Wednesday and Saturday, 10 a.m. to 5 p.m.; Thursday and Friday, 12 noon to 5 p.m. Closed Sunday.
Programs: Summer reading program, preschool story hour.

Wayne County

Bethany Public Library

(717) 253-4349

RR#3, Box 650
Route 670
Honesdale, PA 18431   ⊗ ⧏ ⚲

Hours: Tuesday and Thursday, 3 p.m. to 8 p.m.; fourth Saturday of the month, 9 a.m. to 12 noon. Closed Monday, Wednesday, Friday, and Sunday.
Programs: Summer reading program, crafts, puzzles, games.

Hawley Public Library

(717) 226-4620

103 Main Street   *e-mail: hawpublb@postofficeppd.net*
Hawley, PA 18428   ⊗ ⧏ ⚲

Hours: Monday, 1 p.m. to 4:30 p.m.; Tuesday and Thursday, 10 a.m. to 7:30 p.m.; Wednesday, 10 a.m. to 4:30 p.m.; Friday, 10 a.m. to 4:30 p.m.; Saturday, 10 a.m. to 1 p.m. Closed Sunday.
Programs: Preschool story hour, reading club.

Newfoundland Area Public Library *(717) 676-4518*

Route 507
Newfoundland, PA 18445

Hours: Tuesday and Thursday, 2 p.m. to 4 p.m. and 7 p.m. to 9 p.m.;
Saturday, 10 a.m. to 2 p.m. Closed Monday, Wednesday, Friday,
and Sunday.
Programs: Special children's programs scheduled throughout the
year.

Pleasant Mountain Public Library *(717) 448-2573*

Main Street
Pleasant Mount, PA 18453

Hours: Monday, 4 p.m. to 6 p.m.; Tuesday, 6 p.m. to 8 p.m.; Thursday and Saturday, 1:30 p.m. to 3:30 p.m. Closed Wednesday,
Friday, and Sunday.
Programs: Story hours.

Salem Public Library *(717) 689-0903*

Wimmers Station, Route 191
Hamlin, PA 18427

Hours: Tuesday and Thursday, 10 a.m. to 6 p.m.; Friday, 10 a.m. to
3 p.m. Closed Monday, Wednesday, and Sunday.
Programs: Preschool story hour, summer reading program.

Wayne County Public Library *(717) 253-1220*

1111 Main Street
Honesdale, PA 18431

Hours: Tuesday, Wednesday, and Friday, 10 a.m. to 8 p.m.; Thursday, 10 a.m. to 6 p.m.; Saturday, 10 a.m. to 4 p.m. Closed Sunday
and Monday.
Programs: Summer reading program, story hour.

Pennsylvania Trivia

*Benjamin Franklin was the first
governor of Pennsylvania.*

CHAPTER
7

MOVIES

• •

Hot buttered popcorn, soda, and a movie theater add up to great kid fun. The cinema is a great place to take the kids on a rainy summer day or any day you just want to enjoy a flick together. The listing that follows will assist you in selecting a movie theater to visit. When you call a selected cinema, there will be a recording that lists the movies, show times, and ratings. Sometimes the cost and the discounted rate schedule are mentioned. If that information is not available, scan the local newspaper for a full listing or call the administrative office number provided on the recording. It is also worth mentioning that most theaters will sell tickets in advance and to groups at a discounted rate.

Casino Theater
(717) 839-7831

Route 611, Pocono Blvd.
Mount Pocono, PA 18344

Cinema 6
(717) 251-3456

Route 6 Plaza
Honesdale, PA 18431

East Stroudsburg University Theater
(717) 422-3464
(717) 421-0800

Stroud Hall, Room 113
East Stroudsburg, PA 18301

Note: This theater is open only when the university is in session.

Foxmoor Cinemas
(717) 223-7775

Foxmoor Village
Route 209
Marshalls Creek, PA 18335

Gap Theater
(610) 863-9828

Route 521
Wind Gap, PA 18091

Mahoning Drive-In
(717) 386-9907

Lehighton, PA 18235

Note: This theater is open on a seasonal basis. Kids under 12 are
admitted free.

Milford Theater
(717) 296-9941

Fourth and Katherine Streets
Milford, PA 18337

The Nature Conservancy
(717) 643-7922

Pocono Mountains Office
PO Box 55
Long Pond, PA 18334

Programs: The Conservancy hosts Monday Night at the Movies at
the Tunchannuck Township Municipal Building. Featured topics are on nature.

Pocono Films and Coffee Shop
(717) 421-FILM

88 South Courtland Street
East Stroudsburg, PA 18301

Programs: This theater offers movies for more sophisticated tastes,
often featuring foreign films. You should also watch for some of
the classics to pass through here. A coffee shop is available and
local artists display their work in the theater's foyer.

Sony Theaters
(717) 421-5700

*Stroud Mall*ㅤㅤㅤㅤㅤㅤ(717) 421-5703
*Route 611*ㅤㅤㅤㅤㅤㅤ*www.sony.com*
Stroudsburg, PA 18360

Tri-State Theater
(717) 491-5000

Routes 6 and 209
Milford, PA 18337

CHAPTER

8

MUSEUMS

• •

Museums are a great place to spend a rainy day, or just any day, with your child. Time at a museum can inspire, awaken, and educate your child like nothing else. Whether it's a grouping of artwork or artifacts, children will be impressed with the variety of artistic opportunities only museums can offer.

The staff at the museums are happy to have children visit, but best behavior is always encouraged around the valuable inventory. Some of the museums listed offer interactive exhibits for young hands.

Museums welcome groups, but advance notice is always recommended to assure the best visit possible for the entire group.

Allentown Art Museum   *(610) 432-4333*

PO Box 388   *www.regiononline.com/~atownart/*
5th and Court Streets   ♛ ♿ ♪
Allentown, PA 18105-0388

Description: If you have a budding young architect, you may want
   to expose him or her to the area's only permanent exhibit of
   architecture by Frank Lloyd Wright. In addition to the Wright
   displays, European paintings and sculpture from the 14th
   through 17th century and 200 years of American art are available to enjoy. And don't miss the gem collection—it's a must!
   The museum has exhibits that change from time to time, so call
   ahead for up-to-date showings. If you work up an appetite, there
   is a snack shop available on the premises. Group tours are available by appointment only.

Hours: Tuesday through Saturday, 11 a.m. to 5 p.m.; Sunday, 12 noon to 5 p.m. Closed Mondays and major holidays.

Cost: $3.50 for adults, $3 for senior citizens over 61, $2 for full-time students with an ID, and free for children under 12. If visitors show up on Sunday between the hours of noon and 1 p.m., admission for the entire day is free.

Carbon County Railway Station   *(717) 325-3673*

PO Box 90
Jim Thorpe, PA 18229

Description: The railroad and mine memorabilia exhibited in this authentic railway station focus on the Lehigh Coal and Navigation Company. The Railway Station houses the tourist information center for the town of Jim Thorpe and sells tickets for train rides, too. See Chapter 13 for scheduling information.

Hours: June 1 through October 31: Monday through Friday, 9 a.m. to 4:30 p.m.; Saturday and Sunday, 10 a.m. to 5 p.m. Off-season: daily, 9 a.m. to 4 p.m.

Cost: Free.

Dorflinger Glass Museum   *(717) 253-1185*

PO Box 356   *www.ibcco.com.dorflinger*
Long Ridge Road   *e-mail: dglassmus@aol.com*
White Mills, PA 18473

Description: Over 600 cut-glass pieces from the Dorflinger Glassworks are featured in this museum. The glass pieces are arranged among period antiques. Your child will get wonderful ideas on how to arrange the setting for his or her next tea party. The museum is adjacent to a wildlife sanctuary, which enhances your visits, especially on a sunny day. Nature trails are available for hiking (*see* Chapter 9). Dorflinger also offers a summer concert series (*see* Chapter 11).

Hours: Mid-May through the end of October: Wednesday through Saturday, 10 a.m. to 4 p.m.; Sunday, 1 p.m. to 4 p.m. Closed Monday and Tuesday.

Cost: $3 for adults, $2.50 for senior citizens over 55, $1.50 for children ages 6 to 18, and free for children under 5.

Everhart Museum of Natural History, Science, and Art
(717) 346-7186

1901 Mulberry Street   *www.northeastweb.com/everhart/index.html*
Nay Aug Park   ♟ ♿ ⬡
Scranton, PA 18510-2390

Description: Highlighted in the natural history and science sections of this museum is a model of the prehistoric stegosaurus, an interactive gem lab for the young geologists, and a bird gallery. During warmer weather there is also an active beehive for young explorers. The fine arts section features 19th- and 20th-century American art, plus small European and Folk Art collections. A special attraction in the Everhart Museum is the ethnographic art collection which displays work from some of the various cultures of New Guinea, Africa, and Central America.

Hours: Summer: daily, 12 noon to 5 p.m.; Thursdays, 12 noon to 8 p.m. Columbus Day to Memorial Day: Wednesday through Sunday, 12 noon to 5 p.m.; Thursdays, 12 noon to 8 p.m.

Cost: $3 is the suggested donation for adults, $2 for senior citizens, $1 for children ages 6 to 12, and free for children under 5.

Hooven Mercantile Company Museum   *(717) 325-2248*

41 Susquehanna Street
Jim Thorpe, PA 18229   ♟ ⬡

Description: An incredible HO model train display is waiting for you on the second floor of this building. This two-level model train display has 13 separate model trains that chug along over 1100 feet of track, which winds around 200-plus miniature buildings and about 100 bridges. There is even a night scene that allows the 1000 street lights to shine. The show lasts 30 minutes.

Hours: July through October: Monday through Friday, 12 noon to 4:30 p.m.; Saturday and Sunday, 10 a.m. to 4:30 p.m. November through June: Saturday and Sunday, 12 noon to 4:30 p.m. Closed weekdays.

Cost: $3 for adults, $2 for senior citizens over 64, $1 for children ages 6 to 15, and free for children under 6.

Jem Classic Car Museum

(717) 386-3554

RD #1, Box 120C
Andreas, PA 18211

Description: If a member in your family is interested in various forms of transportation, put your brakes on at the Jem Classic Car Museum. The name of this museum is deceiving because it is so much more than a car museum. The classic cars on display are from 1902 to 1969, although cars are not the only mode of transportation exhibited at this museum. Motorcycles, airplanes, and even an old-fashioned bicycle are available for you to view and learn about. In addition to the vehicles, there is a fairly large doll collection for doll enthusiasts. Call ahead for a private group tour.

Hours: May 30 through October 31: Monday through Friday, 10 a.m. to 4 p.m.; Saturdays, Sundays, and holidays, 12 noon to 4 p.m. Off- season: call ahead for a private group tour.

Cost: $4 for adults; $3.50 for senior citizens, $2.50 for children ages 5 to 12, and free for children under 5.

Kemerer Museum of Decorative Arts

(610) 691-0603

427 North New Street
Bethlehem, PA 18018

Description: As you walk through this museum, period rooms are used to interpret 250 years of folk art, furniture, and fine art. Collections throughout the museum offer a peek into the past. Special children's programming called "Kemerer Kids" is scheduled throughout the year. Kemerer Kids offers children the opportunity to do crafts to learn about history firsthand. A recent event taught kids about the meanings of various flowers during Victorian times and concluded with the assembling of their very own Victorian bouquet. Call to get an updated listing of children's tours and workshops. If you are thinking of having a birthday party or planning a group field trip to the museum, contact the Education Department for the Historic Bethlehem Partnership at (610) 631-0603.

Hours: Tuesday through Sunday, 12 noon to 5 p.m.; closed Mondays and major holidays.

Cost: $3 for adults, $2 for senior citizens, and $7 for the family rate.

Some museums offer children an opportunity to exercise their creativity.
Photo courtesy Fine Arts Discovery Series.

Kittatinny Point Nature Museum   *(908) 496-4458*

⊗ 👫 ♿ 🐾

Bushkill, PA 18324

Description: This small touch museum is located inside one of the
information centers for the Delaware Water Gap National Recreation Area. (Refer to Chapter 9 for more detailed information
on this site.)

Madelon Powers Gallery   *(717) 422-3759*

East Stroudsburg University
Fine and Performing Arts Center
East Stroudsburg, PA 18301   ⊗ 👫 ♿ 🐾

Description: What a great way to become familiar with some of the
local talent. The displays change periodically, so call ahead to
find out what is in store for you. After you are finished at the
gallery, take a tour of the university campus. It is beautiful year-
round.

Hours: Monday through Friday, 1 p.m. to 4:30 p.m.
Cost: Free.

Mary Stolz Doll and Toy Museum   *(717) 588-7566*

McCole Road
Rd #6, Box 6767
East Stroudsburg, PA 18301

Description: Mary Stolz, collector of dolls since 1910, displays her collection of approximately 125 dolls at this museum. This assembling has been maintained by the same family for four generations, and some of the dolls are actually clothed in dresses handmade by Mary Stolz. The dolls are displayed in miniature rooms along with the many toys collected over the years by the family. Cultures from around the world are also featured in the doll displays. The museum shop is as entertaining as the museum. Keep in mind that there is limited wheelchair and stroller accessibility.

Hours: Monday through Saturday, 10:30 a.m. to 6 p.m.; Sunday, 11 a.m. to 5 p.m.

Cost: $2.50 for adults, $1.25 for children ages 3 to 12, and free for children under 3.

Monroe County Environmental Education Center   *(717) 629-3061*

8050 Running Valley Road
Stroudsburg, PA 18360

Description: The environmental education center, described more fully in Chapter 9, displays several interactive exhibits giving children the opportunity to look, touch, and learn about the wildlife that surrounds them. Access to the museum must be scheduled around programming.

Pennsylvania Trivia

The ferris wheel, the typewriter and the Slinky® were all invented in Pennsylvania.

Museum of Indian Culture

(610) 797-2121

Lenni Lenape Historical Society
2825 Fish Hatchery Road
Allentown, PA 18103-9801

www.lenape.org
e-mail: leanape@comcat.com

Description: Start your day at the museum with a slide show geared toward children, which depicts the way Native Americans really lived. When the show concludes children are allowed to interact with the many displays within the museum. They can play music, enjoy Native American games, and smell sweet grass. Your group will also have a chance to visit the Lenape Room and the Inter-Tribal room before you step outside and enjoy the nature trails available to you. In addition, a picnic pavilion is available for families who wish to bring their lunch, and fishing at the nearby hatchery is available for the sports-minded. Contact the center for their special program offerings for school groups and their special-needs programs. They get booked quickly, so call well in advance. The museum also hosts three festivals throughout the year: The Spring Corn Festival in May; Roasting Ears of Corn Food Festival in August; and Time of Thanksgiving in October. Call for exact dates and times.

Hours: Hours for the general public: Wednesday through Sunday, 12 noon to 3 p.m. Groups by appointment: Tuesday through Sunday, 10 a.m. to 4 p.m. Evenings by appointment.

Cost: $2 for adults, $1.50 for children ages 3 to 12, and free for children under 3.

Pennsylvania Fishing Tackle Museum

(717) 775-7237

Pecks Pond Store
Route 402
HC 67, Box 485
Dingmans Ferry, PA 18328

Description: You could get hooked on this place—literally! Fishing memorabilia dating from the 1700s up to the 1950s are on display at this museum. The array of items highlights everything from fly fishing and bait casting to salt water and ice fishing.

Hours: June through August: Monday through Friday, 7 a.m. to 8 p.m.; Saturday and Sunday, 7 a.m. to 9 p.m. September through May: call for hours.

Cost: $4 for adults, $2 for children ages 6 to 12, and free for children under 6.

Pocono Museum Unlimited
(717) 386-3117

517 Ashtown Drive
Route 443
Lehighton, PA 18235

Description: The Pocono Museum Unlimited offers a view of an "O" scale train model. The details in this miniature world are magnificent; there is actually an amusement park that has 16 operating rides and a lake with real fish in it. Shows run every 45 minutes. You must see it to believe it.

Hours: June 1 through Labor Day: Wednesday through Monday, 10:30 a.m. to 4:30 p.m. Closed Tuesday. September through May: Monday and Wednesday through Friday, 12 noon to 4:30 p.m.; Saturday and Sunday, 10:30 a.m. to 4:30 p.m. Closed Tuesday.

Cost: $4 for adults, $3 for senior citizens, $2 for children ages 5 to 12, and free for children under 5.

SMART Discovery Center
(610) 865-5010

511 East Third Street
Bethlehem, PA 18015

Description: This hands-on science center, with 10,000 square feet, features seven different learning areas. The Science Playground, Bodyworks, Discovery Tunnel, The Natural Zone, Workbench, Communication Center, and Arts and Technology areas are all available for experiencing and learning to your heart's content.

Hours: Tuesday through Saturday, 9:30 a.m. to 4:30 p.m.; Sunday, 12 noon to 4:30 p.m. Closed Mondays.

Cost: $4.50 for adults, $4 for senior citizens over 62, $3.50 for children ages 4 to 12, and free for children under 3.

Pennsylvania Trivia

Pennsylvania gets its name from
Penn's Woods (after Admiral Penn).

Art Councils

The area Art Councils serve as a resource for artists as well as community members to reference the variety of cultural opportunities in the region. Memberships are available and offer benefits in terms of advance notice and discounts to events.

Cultural Council   *(717) 826-6111*

Public Square
Suite 804
Wilkes-Barre, PA 18707

Lehigh Valley Arts Council   *(610) 861-0678*

PO Box 20591
Lehigh Valley, PA 18002-0591

Monroe County Arts Council   *(717) 476-4460*

556 Main Street
Stroudsburg, PA 18360

Pennsylvania Trivia

At one time, the Poconos was the second most popular tourist destination in America, surpassed only by the Niagara Falls.

In addition to enjoying the splash of autumn color, have the fun of harvesting your own produce. Photo courtesy Pocono Mountains Vacation Bureau, Inc.

CHAPTER
9

NATURE

● ●

The lakes, streams, and wildlife that coexist with the human habitat can be more fully appreciated when families are educated about their environment. Consequently, it is no surprise that the Pocono region offers many opportunities to learn about its untamed surroundings. Many nature programs, hiking trails, and outdoor adventures can be enjoyed by contacting one of the area's Environmental Education Centers, Wildlife Rehabilitation Centers, or Ranger Stations at the national and state parks near you.

Another great way to enjoy the outdoors as a family is to plan a day to pick your own fruit, pumpkins, or Christmas trees at nearby farms.

Whether your family takes advantage of one of the many programs offered at area Environmental Education Centers, Wildlife Rehabilitation Centers, and national and state parks, or feasts on nature's bounty at a pick-your-own farm, your clan is sure to have a good time. It's only natural!

ENVIRONMENTAL EDUCATION CENTERS

All Environmental Education Centers promote environmental awareness by offering a full calendar of events. Listed below are the nature centers in the Pocono region. Programs at the centers vary. Some of the centers have museums, others have nature trails or birding opportunities, yet all of them offer exciting and educational programs for children and their parents to enjoy. Contact any of the centers listed below to receive a newsletter and inquire about their programs. Most of the centers offer memberships for families or individuals that include special benefits and discounts. Preregistration is required or at least recommended for all programs.

Carbon County Environmental Education Center
(717) 645-8597

625 Lentz Trail
Jim Thorpe, PA 18210

Description: The ongoing children's programs include the "Creepy Crawlers" and the Ranger Rick Club. These programs run on a monthly basis throughout the year to explore nature topics that are age appropriate. The staff also runs off-site programs for groups and organizations. The facilities include nature trails, a boardwalk trail, a bird blind on Mauch Chunk Lake, nature displays, and an outdoor picnic pavilion. The center also has nonreleasable birds of prey for educational purposes.

Hours: Monday through Friday, 8 a.m. to 4 p.m.

Cost: Free to families taking a self-guided tour of the facility. A nominal donation is suggested for all on-site programs. Group presentations have a fee that varies with each program. Call in advance for reservations.

The Dorflinger-Suydam Wildlife Sanctuary
(717) 253-1185

Long Ridge Road   *www.ibcco.com/dorflinger*
White Mills, PA 18473   *e-mail: dglassmus@aol.com*

Description: Situated on the grounds of former glassmaker Christian Dorflinger's vacation home, the 600-acre wildlife sanctuary is threaded with nature trails. After you meander through the nature trails, consider visiting the Dorflinger Glass Museum (*see* Chapter 8) or staying for one of the outdoor summer concerts (*see* Chapter 11).

Hours: Dawn to dusk.

Cost: Free.

Pennsylvania Trivia

The state flower is the mountain laurel.

Lacawac Wildlife Sanctuary   *(717) 689-9494*

RD #1, Box 518
Lake Ariel, PA 18436

Description: The sanctuary is a field station for research and a training facility for students. Registered as a National Natural Landmark and National Historic Site, the facility provides a variety of programs for the public. Families should wear hiking boots or comfortable shoes to enjoy the nature trails. It is recommended that you call to receive a schedule of their summer programs and hours of operation.

Hours: Vary with the season. Call to inquire.

Cost: Varies with the program.

Monroe County Environmental Education Center   *(717) 629-3061*

8050 Running Valley Road
Stroudsburg, PA 18360

Description: Year-round environmental education programs are provided for all age groups. The preschool and young adult programs are excellent. This center has three sites throughout the Pocono region that enable the staff to illustrate a variety of topics.

Kettle Creek Wildlife Sanctuary
Bartonsville, PA

Description: The sanctuary is a 120-acre preserve with a pond, picnic tables, and over 1½ miles of well-marked trails for public use. The environmental education center is located at this site. There are two classrooms, a resource library, a bookstore, and interactive nature displays.

Hours: Monday through Friday, 8:30 a.m. to 4:30 p.m.; Saturday, 9 a.m. to 4 p.m. Trails are open dawn to dusk.

Cost: Varies with the program; nature trails are free.

Meesing Site
Marshalls Creek, PA

Description: Swamp, streams, a pond, and a variety of habitats are available to the public on this 100-acre tract of land. There are four miles of nature trails. The highlight of this center is the maple forest that houses a Sugar Shack used to produce maple syrup. Every March the center has a program for families to demonstrate the tapping of the maple trees and syrup production. Then everyone gets to taste the sweet syrup on pancakes.

Hours: Dawn to dusk

Cost: Varies with the program. Nature trails are free.

Cranberry Bog
Tannersville, PA

Description: Access to the bog is limited to registrants of nature programs. Families and groups are invited to take a closer look at the bog habitat by strolling on the floating boardwalk.

Hours: Accessible only during nature center programs.

Cost: Varies with the program.

The Nature Conservancy
(717) 643-7922

Pocono Mountains Office
PO Box 55
Long Pond, PA 18334

Description: Events for children and families are offered here throughout the year, although scheduling really heats up during the summer. Some of their best events include the Kids Conservation Corps, a popular program with the young ones, and Monday Night at the Movies, a film presentation hosted by the Nature Conservancy. Call the center for details. Nature trails are open to the public.

Hours: Monday through Friday, 9 a.m. to 4 a.m. Trails are open dawn to dusk.

Cost: Varies with the program. Nature trails are free.

Pike County Conservation District
(717) 226-8220

HC #6, Box 6770
Route 402
Hawley, PA 18428

Description: A variety of evening programs and special events are available. Call to get current information.

Hours: Monday through Friday, 8 a.m. to 4:30 p.m.

Cost: Varies with the program.

Pocono Environmental Education Center (717) 828-2319

RR 2, Box 1010
Dingmans Ferry, PA 18328

Description: Visit the 38-acre campus with residential facilities and access to 200,000 acres of public lands, plus a 39-acre land preserve of The Nature Conservancy. The staff offers day camp and special weekend family camping programs. Nature trails are open to the public. See if you can find the fossil pit. Another family favorite is the center's Nature Study Weekend.
Hours: Daily, 9 a.m. to 5 p.m. Trails are open dawn to dusk.
Cost: Varies with the program. Nature trails are free.

WILDLIFE REHABILITATION CENTERS

Wildlife Rehabilitation Centers are staffed by volunteers who have an infectious love for wildlife. Most of the time the staff is on call year-round, 24 hours a day, in case of a wildlife emergency. If you ever find a wounded or orphaned animal, these are the folks that you call. They will give you advice on how to handle the situation. In the event that your family finds an animal in distress, it is important that any handling of the animal is kept to a minimum, and you call for help right away. These centers are funded by donations and memberships. If you have an opportunity to visit the facility or must drop off an animal, a donation would be greatly appreciated. Staff members at these facilities are usually eager to speak to groups of school children. Programs may be offered on- or off-site.

Delaware Valley Raptor Center (717) 296-6025

RD #2, Box 9335
Milford, PA 18337

Description: This center is dedicated to the rehabilitation of all injured or orphaned raptors (hawks, eagles, falcons, owls). Educational programs and tours are available on- and off-site and must be scheduled in advance. Membership allows you several privileges, including the ability to visit the center on a regular basis. Call the Raptor Center to inquire about memberships and group programs.

Hours: Members only. April through October: the last Sunday of the month, 1 p.m. to 4 p.m.
Cost: Varies with the program. Donations are accepted.

Pennsylvania Raptor and Wildlife Association
(717) 897-6659

7 Allegheny Road
Mount Bethel, PA 18343

Description: This center is home to many injured and orphaned wildlife and raptors. Mountain lions, cougars, bald eagles, wolves, and golden eagles are all cared for at this facility. The staff is available for group presentations on- and off-site to discuss the biology and ecology of the animals native to the Pocono region. Contact the center for membership and group program information.
Hours: Members only, the first Sunday of the month, 12:30 p.m. to 4 p.m.
Cost: $150.00 per program; 40-child limit per on-site presentation.

Pocono Wildlife Rehabilitation Center
(717) 894-8850

383 Green Road
Tobyhanna, PA 18466

Description: This center is a place where injured and orphaned animals can be cared for until they can be returned to the wild. The staff is available for presentations to groups.
Hours: Call to inquire.
Cost: Donations are appreciated.

Pennsylvania Trivia

Pennsylvania has more than 8 million acres of preserved land. At any point in the state you are within 25 miles from a state park. The Pocono region is home to seven of the state parks as well as a very large national park.

NATIONAL AND STATE PARK NATURE PROGRAMS

The Pocono area is fortunate to have a variety of national and state parks. The national and state parks employ rangers or naturalists to offer summer nature programs to campers or to anyone who would like to become more familiar with their forest friends. For more information on all the activities and amenities that are available at each location, refer to Chapter 10.

Delaware Water Gap National Recreation Area
(717) 588-2451

Bushkill, PA 18324

www.nps.gov/dewa
e-mail: from web site
♨ ♟ ♿*(center only)*

Description: The Delaware Water Gap National Recreation Area offers several programs throughout the summer, including Terrace Talks, a Junior Naturalist, and a Junior Ranger program. There is also a slide show and a touch museum at each site listed below. Call the visitor centers for hours and program availability.

Bushkill Visitor Center (717) 588-7044
Kittatinny Point Visitor Center (908) 496-4458

Hours: Vary with site and program.
Cost: Free.

State Park Nature Programs

The summer is the time to catch the nature programs offered by the Rangers at the state parks in the area. Call the park offices listed below to discover the selection of nature offerings near you.

Beltzville State Park
(215) 377-0045

RD #3, Box 242
Lehighton, PA 18235

Hickory Run State Park
(717) 443-9991

RD #1, Box 81
White Haven, PA 18661

Promised Land State Park
(717) 676-3428

RD #1, Box 96
Greentown, PA 18426

Tobyhanna State Park
(717) 894-8336

PO Box 387
Tobyhanna, PA 18466

HARVESTING

Spend the afternoon picking your harvest and the rest of the day eating it! The pick-your-own fruit and vegetable farms provide a fun and wholesome way to spend time together. Another festive family activity is selecting the perfect Christmas tree. Some of the farms below offer festivals and other activities at various times throughout the year. Refer to Chapter 5 to make sure you don't miss a great time. Call first for up-to-date information.

Carbon County

Graver Orchards
(610) 377-0769

1600 Owl Creek Road
Lehighton, PA 18235

Harvest: Strawberries (June), blueberries (July), raspberries (July to frost)

Old Homestead Tree Farm
(610) 381-3582

RR #2, Box 175
Kunkletown, PA 18085

Harvest: Pumpkins (October), Christmas trees

Semmel Farm
(610) 377-1189

1146 West Lizard Creek Road
Lehighton, PA 18235

Harvest: Blueberries (July to August), Christmas trees

Walker's Tree Farm and Pumpkin Patch   *(610) 377-1829*

308 Spruce Street
Lehighton, PA 18235

Harvest: Pumpkins (October), Christmas trees

Monroe County

AJ's Vegetables and Produce   *(717) 424-2647*

Routes 33 and 209
Snydersville, PA

Harvest: Pumpkins (late September to October)

Picking apples right from the tree is better than the grocery store any day.

Gould's Produce   *(717) 992-5615*

Frable Road
Box 126
Brodheadsville, PA 18322

Harvest: Strawberries (June to July), pumpkins (October)

Heckman Orchards   *(717) 629-1191*

RR #3, Box 2469
Effort, PA 18330

Harvest: Strawberries (June to July), sour cherries (July), apples (September to October), pumpkins (September to October)

Heller's Farm Market   *(717) 828-2105*

Route 209
Bushkill, PA

Harvest: Strawberries (June)

Hidden Valley Farms   *(717) 421-9865*

RR #5, Box 5431
Franklin Hill Road
East Stroudsburg, PA 18301

Harvest: Christmas trees
Programs: Hayrides are offered during the holiday season, weather permitting

Lyle's Produce   *(610) 381-3661*

Weir Lake Road
Brodheadsville, PA 18322

Harvest: Strawberries (June)

Newswanger's Tree Farm   *(610) 381-3184*

RR #1, Box 1718
Saylorsburg, PA 18353

Harvest: Christmas trees

Pike County

Paupack Blueberry Farm

(717) 226-9702
(717) 226-4454

HCR Box 47
Paupack, PA 18451

Harvest: Blueberries (July to August)

Wayne County

Bertram's Orchard

(717) 253-4105

RD #3, Box 105
Honesdale, PA 18431

Harvest: Blueberries (July to August), pumpkins (September to October), cider making (September to Thanksgiving; call to inquire)

Pennsylvania Trivia

Pocono is an Indian word meaning "stream between two mountains."

Many state parks have lakes that let you include sailing as part of a day's fun. Photo by Jim McElholm.

CHAPTER
10

PARKS

• •

STATE AND NATIONAL PARKS

For a family that loves the outdoors, the Delaware Water Gap National Recreation Area and area state parks are a treasure trove. In fact, there is so much to do that I would recommend calling ahead to get information in order to plan your excursion. If you are unable to plan ahead, stop in at one of the facilities listed below and pick up one of the maps or speak with a Ranger. All parks are required to be wheelchair accessible. Some parks offer more wheelchair facilities than others, so it is advised that inquiries are made ahead of time to avoid disappointment. Please remember that no pets or alcohol are allowed in any of the parks. If you're planning an overnight camp out, remember the campsites need to be reserved in advance by the calling the park office. As with any outdoor activity in the summer, bring sunscreen and bug spray.

Fishing and hunting regulations are strictly enforced in Pennsylvania. Fishing licenses are required by individuals 16 years of age and older. Fishing licenses may be obtained in most bait and tackle shops in the region. Hunting licenses are required as well by hunters 16 years of age or older, and may be purchased at most sporting goods shops.

State Park Service Web Site: Get the latest information on what's happening within the park system at www.bcnr.state.pa.us.

National Park Service Web Site: Up-to-date information on the Delaware Water Gap National Recreation Area is available at www.nps.gov//dewg.

State Parks

Beltzville State Park   *(610) 377-0045*

RD #3, Box 242   *e-mail: beltzville.sp@al.dcnr.state.pa.us*
Lehighton, PA 18235

Area: 2972 acres
Facilities: Picnicking, snack bar
Amenities: Playground, playfield, beach, hiking trails
Activities: Fishing, boating, canoeing, rentals, ice skating, cross-country skiing, sledding
Special Things: Nature talks, snowmobile trails, hunting, covered bridge

Big Pocono State Park   *(717) 894-8336*

c/o Tobyhanna State Park   e-mail: tobyhanna.sp@al.dcnr.state.pa.us
PO Box 387 Tobyhanna, PA 18466-0387

Area: 1306 acres
Facilities: Picnicking
Amenities: Hiking trails, bike paths, bridle paths
Activities: Cross-country skiing, sledding
Special Things: Hunting

Gouldsboro State Park   *(717) 894-8336*

c/o Tobyhanna State Park PO   e-mail: tobyhanna.sp@al.dcnr.state.pa.us
Box 387
Tobyhanna, PA 18466-0387

Area: 2800 acres
Facilities: Picnicking
Amenities: Playfield, beach, hiking trails
Activities: Fishing, boating, canoeing, rentals, ice skating, cross-country skiing
Special Things: Snowmobile trails, hunting

Pennsylvania Trivia

The first Boy Scout camp in the United States was established at LakeTeedyuskung in Milford, Pike County.

Snowmobile trails in many of the area parks are a way to experience the Pocono Mountains in the winter. Photo courtesy Pocono Mountains Vacation Bureau, Inc.

Hickory Run State Park   *(717) 443-0400*

RD #1, Box 81   e-mail: hickoreyrun.sp@al.dcnr.state.pa.us
White Haven, PA 18661

Area: 15,483 acres
Facilities: Picnicking, snack bar
Amenities: Playground, playfield, beach, hiking trails, snowmobile trails, tent camping
Activities: Fishing, ice skating, cross-country skiing, sledding
Special Things: Boulder field, nature programs, hunting

Lehigh Gorge State Park   *(717) 443-0400*

c/o Hickory Run State Park   e-mail: hickoreyrun.sp@al.dcnr.state.pa.us
RD #1, Box 81 Whitehaven, PA 18661

Area: 4548 acres
Amenities: Hiking trails, bike paths
Activities: Fishing, boating, canoeing, cross-country skiing
Special Things: Whitewater rafting

Promised Land State Park   *(717) 676-3428*

RD #1, Box 96   *e-mail: promland.sp@a1.state.dcnr.state.pa.us*
Greentown, PA 18426

Area: 2971 acres
Facilities: Picnicking
Amenities: Playground, playfield, beach, hiking trails, nearby bridle and biking trails, tent camping, cabins
Activities: Fishing, boating, canoeing, ice skating, cross-country skiing
Special Things: Nature programs, snowmobile trails

Tobyhanna State Park   *(717) 894-8336*

PO Box 387   *e-mail tobyhanna.sp@al.dcnr.state.pa.us*
Tobyhanna, PA 18466-0387

Area: 5440 acres
Facilities: Picnicking
Amenities: Playground, playfield, beach, hiking trails, bike path, snowmobile trails
Activities: Fishing, boating, canoeing, ice skating, cross-country skiing
Special Things: Hunting

National Parks

Delaware Water Gap National
Recreation Area   *(717) 588-2451*

Bushkill, PA 18324   *e-mail: dewa_interpretation@nps.gov*
www.nps.gov/dewa

Area: 70,000 acres
Facilities: Picnicking
Amenities: Beach, hiking trails, snowmobile trails, tenting
Activities: Fishing, boating, canoeing, cross-country skiing
Special Things: Nature talks, hunting, information center

Delaware Water Gap National Recreation Area Visitor's Center

(717) 588-7044

Bushkill

Special Things: Bookstore, information center

Delaware Water Gap National Recreation Area Visitor's Center

(908) 496-4458

Kittatinny Point

Facilities: Picnicking
Amenities: Beach, hiking trails
Activities: Fishing, boating, canoeing, cross-country skiing
Special Things: Nature museum, information for rock climbing, bookstore

AMUSEMENT PARKS

Nothing says summer more than a day at an amusement park. The Poconos has several wonderful places that give you and your child a day of fun to remember. It is always recommended to call ahead to reserve picnic pavilions, check rates and hours, and make arrangements for groups.

Camelback Alpine Slide

(717) 629-1661

PO Box 168   *www.silo.com/poconos/camelback/home.htm*
Tannersville, PA 18372

Description: This summer-season outdoor water park includes an alpine slide, swimming pool, water slide, and lots of other wet and wild adventures. There are also go-carts, bumper boats, amusements, and miniature golf for the family to enjoy. There are height requirements on some of the attractions.

Hours: May through mid-June: Sunday and Saturday, 10 a.m. to 5:30 p.m. Mid-June through Labor Day: Monday through Friday, 10 a.m. to 5:30 p.m.; Saturday, Sunday, and July 4th, 10 a.m. to 6 p.m. September through mid-October: Saturday and Sunday, 11 a.m. to 4 p.m.

Cost: May to Labor Day: $19.95 for adults, $14.95 for juniors (33" to 47"). After Labor Day: $14.95 for adults, $9.95 for juniors. Season Combo Pass: $150. Pool Pass: $75.

Take a dip in one of the wet and wild water parks available in the Pocono region. Photo courtesy Pocono Mountains Vacation Bureau, Inc.

Carousel Water and Fun Park   *(717) 729-7532*

PO Box 5
Beach Lake, PA 18405

Description: Miniature golf, go-carts, bumper boats, water slides, kiddie cars, a batting range, and arcade await you.

Hours: Memorial Day through Labor Day: daily, 11 a.m. to 10 p.m. September: weekends only. Call for hours.

Cost: An all-day pass is $16 for people 45" and over, and $10 for people under 45". Pay as you go prices range from $1.25 to $2.50 per activity.

Costa's Family Fun Park   *(717) 226-8585*

RT #6, Lords Valley
PO Box 488
Hawley, PA 18428

Description: When your family is all revved up with no place to go, try Costa's Family Fun Park. The miniature golf, driving range, batting cages, and arcade will whet their appetites for the go-carts and kiddie cars and finally some ice cream. Don't forget the toddlers. This family park has a Kiddie Land equipped with ball pit, tunnels, and toddler toys. The batting cages and Kiddie Land are under cover for a rainy day.

Hours: Memorial Day through Labor Day: daily, 11 a.m. to 12 midnight. Call for off-season hours.

Cost: $2.50 to $5.50 is the price range for individual activities.

Dorney Park and Wildwater Kingdom   *(800) FUN-TIME*

3830 Dorney Park Road   *(610) 395-2000*
Allentown, PA 18104

Description: This 200-acre entertainment complex with over 100 rides and attractions is home to one of the country's tallest wooden roller coasters (there are three roller coasters in all), water plunge ride, carousel, race cars, and miniature golf, to name a few attractions. For the tots, there is Berenstein Bear Country and specially designed interactive attractions. Wildwater Kingdom has over a dozen water rides and two special tot spots—Kid's Cove and Lollipop Lagoon. Food is available in both parks, and picnic facilities are located outside of the park.

Hours: Park: June through August and on weekends from Labor Day through October: Monday through Friday, 10 a.m. to 10 p.m.; Saturday and Sunday, 10 a.m. to 11 p.m. Water Park: Memorial Day through June: daily, 10 a.m. to 5 p.m. June through September: daily, 10 a.m. to 7 p.m.

Cost: Including both parks: $24.95 for adults (48" tall and over), $4.95 for senior citizens (over 59) and children (under 48" tall), free for children under 3. After 5 p.m. it's $10.50. For a two-day pass: $32.95 for adults, $9.90 for senior citizens and children. Admission to Dorney Park only is $19.95. Call for off-season rates. Parking is $3.

Fun and Games   *(717) 253-9111*

Plaza Center Mall, Route 6
Honesdale, PA 18431

Description: Fun and Games has indoor mini-golf, bumper cars, and an arcade.

Hours: Memorial Day through Labor Day: Monday through Thursday, 11 a.m. to 10 p.m.; Friday, 11 a.m. to 11 p.m.; Saturday, 10 a.m. to 11 p.m.; Sunday, 10 a.m. to 10 p.m. Off-season: Monday through Thursday, 12 noon to 9 p.m.; Friday and Saturday, 11 a.m. to 9 p.m.; Sunday, 11 a.m. to 9 p.m.

Cost: $5, $6, and $7 bags of tokens. Group rates offered for 10 or more.

Go-Kart Rides   *(717) 223-6299*

Route 209, Liberty Square
Marshalls Creek, PA 18335

Description: Small motorized go-carts that you and your child can ride on a track.

Hours: April through November: hours vary with season. Call ahead.

Cost: $3 per ride or $10 for four rides.

Pennsylvania Trivia

The state dog is the Great Dane.

Golf Plus Park

(717) 689-4996

Box 65C, Golf Park Drive
Lake Ariel, PA 18436

Description: Situated within the grand view of the Lake Wallenpaupack region, this is the country's largest bumper boat lagoon. You can also enjoy two monster mini-golf ranges, a super Grand Prix Go-Kart Track, a driving range, an arcade, and a snack bar. Golf Plus Park is also home to the lovable Buttons the Bear. On weekends, Buttons is happy to offer train rides to all the visitors.

Hours: April through October: daily, 10 a.m. to 11 p.m.
Cost: $3.00 to $5.50 per activity.

Imagination Zone

(717) 992-5035

PO Box 780
Route 209, Monroe Plaza
Brodheadsville, PA 18322

Description: This indoor playground with slides, ball pits, and tunnels is a wonderful place to play when you can't go outside. Wacky Wednesday offers a special play all day price of $3.99.

Hours: Monday through Thursday, 10 a.m. to 8 p.m.; Friday and Saturday, 10 a.m. to 9 p.m.; Sunday, 11 a.m. to 8 p.m.
Cost: $5.99 for children ages 3 to 12 years, $3.99 for children ages 1 to 2 years, and free for children under 12 months.

King of Swing

(717) 424-9045

River Road
Minisink Hill, PA 18341

Description: This family-owned play park features batting cages, a miniature-golf range, and an inside arcade and ice cream stand.

Hours: Memorial Day through Labor Day: daily, 10 a.m. to 10 p.m. September through October: daily, 3 p.m. to 7 p.m.
Cost: Miniature golf is $4 for adults and $3 for children. Batting cages are $1.25 for fourteen pitches.

Pocono Go-Karts

(717) 620-0820

Route 611
Bartonsville, PA 18321

Description: This facility includes go-carts, batting cages, and miniature golf, as well as a driving range. A trip here guarantees something for everyone.

Hours: Memorial Day through Labor Day: daily, 10 a.m. to 10 p.m.

Cost: Go-carts are $3 a ride or $10 for four rides. Miniature Golf is $4 for adults and $2.50 for children. Batting cages are $1 for a dozen balls.

Have a ball at Shawnee Place Play and Water Park. Photo courtesy Pocono Mountains Vacation Bureau, Inc.

Shawnee Place Play and Water Park   *(717) 421-7231*

Shawnee Mountain Ski Area
Shawnee-on-Delaware, PA 18356

Description: Water slides, pools, a ball pit, and magic shows are offered here. Every Tuesday is Grandparent's Day—grandparents admitted free! Picnicking is allowed with all admissions.
Hours: Memorial Day through Labor Day: daily, 10 a.m. to 5 p.m.
Cost: $10 for general admission, $5 for spectators, and free for children 40" and under.

Thunder Creek Quarry   *(717) 223-7177*

Mountain Manor Inn
Marshalls Creek, PA 18355

Description: This indoor and outdoor family fun center is home to go-carts, bumper boats, miniature golf, kiddie karts, in-line skating, an arcade, plus an on-site snack bar. The facility opened its doors in the spring of 1997 and is already busy hosting birthday parties and offering group packages. Check this one out.
Hours: Open year-round. Memorial Day through Labor Day: Sunday through Thursday, 11 a.m. to 10 p.m.; Friday and Saturday, 11 a.m. to 11 p.m. Call for off-season hours.
Cost: $2 to $5 per activity (pay as you go).

Time Out Family Amusement Center   *(717) 424-8692*

Stroud Mall
Route 611
Stroudsburg, PA 18360

Description: This indoor arcade, with many games and several stationary rides, is conveniently located near a movie theater. A dynamic duo sure to help pass a rainy afternoon quickly.
Hours: Monday through Saturday, 10 a.m. to 9 p.m.; Sunday, 10 a.m. to 6 p.m.
Cost: Tokens must be purchased for each game.

Families have a chance to meet the artists after performances. Photo courtesy Fine Arts Discovery Series.

CHAPTER
11

PERFORMING ARTS

• •

The curtain goes up. Onstage is a favorite storybook character. Your family is mesmerized by the show, as the classic tale you have read to your child comes to life. Or you listen to concert music so bold you can feel the drums down in your stomach. A visit to one of the performing art centers will allow you and your family, for at least a couple of hours, to be suspended in time. Once you visit a live performance, your children will be yelling, "Encore, encore!"

Cultivating an appreciation for the arts is never wasted time. In addition to viewing live performances, this section also lists several classes that allow parent and child to enjoy time together.

MUSIC

Allentown Symphony Hall   (610) 432-6715

23 North 6th Street   *e-mail: asymph@aol.com*
Allentown, PA 18101   ♦♦♦ ᕕ ᕗ

If music is your family's thing, this symphony hall offers a variety of classical music in a family concert series of five concerts during a season. Once a year the Allentown Symphony hosts an interactive performance designed specifically for school groups and families. Call for an updated schedule of events.

Dorflinger Glass Museum: Outdoor Music Series
(717) 253-1185

PO Box 356
Long Ridge Road
White Mills, PA 18473

www.ibcco.com.dorflinger
e-mail: dglassmus@aol.com

The Festival Committee of Dorflinger presents a summer music series. Outdoor concerts are performed on Saturdays at 6 p.m. You must call in advance for tickets. Also, call on the day of performance after 3 p.m. to find out if the concert is to be rescheduled due to weather. Couple this trip with a visit to the Dorflinger Glass Museum (*see* Chapter 8) or take a stroll on a trail at the on-site wildlife sanctuary (*see* Chapter 9) to make this trip complete.

Fine Arts Discovery Series: Concerts for Children
(717) 476-3237

PO Box 1126
Stroudsburg, PA 18360

Performances sponsored by the Fine Arts Discovery Series (FADS) are geared directly toward children's interests. Families have the opportunity to experience a live performance and are given a chance to meet and talk with the artist. Performances are usually held at the Stroudsburg High School Auditorium on Main Street in Stroudsburg, although the show location is subject to change depending on the performance. Most shows provide a workshop prior to the performance for families to interact with the artists and learn more about the content of the show. This opportunity offers the children a better understanding and appreciation of the performance. Four concerts are provided in a series at a family rate, although families may purchase tickets on a show by show basis.

Kindermusik Beginnings
(717) 629-7888

PO Box 150, Doll Drive
Reeders, PA 18352

This program is geared for parent and child (18 months to 3 years old). The 15-week course provides an opportunity for parents and children to sing, dance, play instruments, and have fun while exploring the joy of music. If your toddler takes to this class, you may consider enrollment in Growing with Kindermusik (ages 3½ to

4½ years old) or Kindermusik for the Young Child (ages 4½ to 7 years old). The classes for the older children allow the parents to participate in the last fifteen minutes of every class. All class costs include materials. Class sizes are limited, so sign up early.

Lehigh Valley Chamber Orchestra *(610) 266-8555*

1 Center Square, Suite 201
Allentown, PA 18101

This professional orchestra offers several concerts throughout the year. Families wishing to enjoy what the chamber has to offer may subscribe to an annual concert series, which runs from September through May.

Music for Little People *(717) 424-6386*

482 Penn Estates
East Stroudsburg, PA 18301

Music for Little People provides a two-tier Kindermusik curriculum. Kindermusik Beginnings is for children ages 18 months to 3 years old, and is a parent/child class that demonstrates the joys of learning songs, dances, and playing instruments. Graduates as well as new enrollees may participate in the next level, Growing with Kindermusik, which is geared for 3½ to 4½ year olds. Parents are able to participate in the last fifteen minutes of every class. Preregistration is required for both classes.

Northeastern Pennsylvania Philharmonic *(717) 457-8301*

Box 71   *www/nepaphil.com*
Avoca, PA 18641   *e-mail: info.nepaphil.com*

The Northeastern Pennsylvania Philharmonic offers a variety of musical entertainment from September through May. Classical and pops musical selections are offered in various subscriber packages. The Family Series includes a classical and pops concert as well as a holiday concert providing a wonderful mix for your family to enjoy. Concerts are held either at the FM Kirby Center or the Scranton Cultural Center, both located in Scranton. Matinees are scheduled to accommodate early bedtimes, too. Call to discover what the latest concert season has to offer.

Pennsylvania Sinfonia Orchestra   *(610) 434-7811*

1524 Linden Street
Allentown, PA 18102

A variety of classical and contemporary concerts are performed throughout the year by the Pennsylvania Sinfonia Orchestra. The concert series is held on Saturday nights at 7:30 p.m., and the concert locations vary although most are held at Symphony Hall in Allentown, Pennsylvania. When inquiring about concert packages, make sure you ask about the Be Our Guest music student program. The Be Our Guest program offers preconcert interaction with the conductor as well as postconcert receptions, making the entire concert experience affordable and educational. The Pennsylvania Sinfona can also provide in-school programs including Composer in Your Classroom and New Sounds/Old Instruments.

Presbyterian Church of the Mountain   *(717) 476-0345*

Main Street
Delaware Water Gap, PA 18327

Take a picnic dinner and enjoy an outdoor concert on Sundays from June through August beginning at 6 p.m. This series of summer entertainment provides an opportunity to listen to regional jazz, country, and blues performers. There is no charge for the performance. Just relax on the lawn and enjoy.

Shawnee Mountain Summer Concert Series   *(717) 421-5093*

Shawnee Inn and Golf Resort
River Road
Shawnee on Delaware, PA 18356

Grab a lawn chair or a blanket and head down to the lawn by the river for a free musical concert at Shawnee Inn. Bringing your own refreshments and snacks is strictly prohibited; some items, however, are available at Shawnee during the concert. Make it a family event every Tuesday night at 7 p.m. during July and August.

TELEVISION

Kids Express TV Show   *(610) 377-4060*

Channel 13
Blue Ridge Cable Television, Inc.
936 Elm Street
Lehighton, PA 18235   ⊛ 🖊

Tune into Channel 13 for guided tours of fun and educational places. Tours range from the Baltimore Aquarium to kid-friendly places in the Poconos.

Hours: Monday and Tuesday, 3:30 p.m.; Thursday, 10:30 a.m.; Saturday and Sunday, 10 a.m.

THEATER

Fine Arts and Performing Center: Theater and Concert Hall   *(717) 422-3759*

East Stroudsburg University   *www.esu.edu*
East Stroudsburg, PA 18301   *e-mail: from web site*
                                            🚻 ♿ 🖊

It would be a good idea to contact the university from time to time to get the schedule of the various concerts and theater productions. The center makes it a point to host a children's production annually in the fall.

FM Kirby Center for the Performing Arts   *(717) 826-1100*

PO Box 486   *Group Sales: (717) 823-4599*
71 Public Square
Wilkes-Barre, PA 18703-0486   🚻 ♿ 🖊

In addition to offering first-rate productions for the general public, the FM Kirby Center has a fantastic Children's Theater Festival. Any ticket holder during the festival may take part in Playworks at no additional charge. Playworks is an area dedicated to hands-on arts and crafts activities and nonstop entertainment by storytellers. The area also features a puppet theater and musical performances. Teachers will be pleased to know that study guides are available prior to the festival. If the times and dates of the festival don't fit into your schedule, check out the general programs for some year-round family fun.

Little Theater of Wilkes-Barre   *(717) 823-1875*

537 North Main Street
Wilkes-Barre, PA 18702

This local community theater hosts four productions a year. In addition to the shows, the troop dedicates its summer workshop to children's theater. Contact the theater for a full schedule of events.

Mauch Chunk Opera House   *(717) 325-4439*

14 West Broadway Street
Jim Thorpe, PA 18229

One of the most popular events at the Opera House is the line-up at the annual Laurel Blossom Festival (*see* Chapter 5). Yet year-round you may be able to catch some good family entertainment. A variety of family shows are held, including Christmas shows and, most recently, a production of *James and the Giant Peach.*

Pocono Playhouse   *(717) 595-7456*

Playhouse Lane, PA Hwy. 390
PO Box 207
Mountainhome, PA 18342

The summer heats up the stage with children's theater at the Pocono Playhouse. Saturday mornings in the summer are the best time to take the children to a live production of *Little Red Riding Hood, Sleeping Beauty,* or other classics. While you're there, look at the full schedule of events for an evening with or without the kids.

Ritz Company Playhouse   *(717) 226-9752*

512 Keystone Street
Hawley, PA 18428   ♦♦♦ ☰ ☎

Tucked away in the quaint town of Hawley is the Ritz Company Playhouse. Open only during the summer, this theater provides musicals, comedies, and community theater. Call for up-to-date information.

Shawnee Playhouse   *(717) 421-5093*

River Road
Shawnee-on-Delaware, PA 18356   ♔♔♔ ⬧ ♞

Situated in the charming town of Shawnee-on-the-Delaware is the Shawnee Playhouse. Destroyed by fire many years ago, the theater has risen from the ashes and is better than ever. Every summer the playhouse provides quality children's theater. Not only do you get to enjoy live theater, but the Shawnee players make a point of signing the children's programs after the performance. Additionally, full-length musicals and plays are staged throughout the year.

State Theater Center for the Arts   *(610) 252-3132*

453 Northampton Street   *(800) 999-STATE*
Easton, PA 18042   *www.statetheatre.org*
                                         e-mail: from web site
                                              🎂 ♔♔♔ ⬧ ♞

Give your kids the experience of going to Broadway without the hassle. The State Theater provides a large selection of top-notch entertainment year-round. Special children's productions are scheduled throughout the year; *Where The Wild Things Are* and *Laura Ingalls-Wilder: Life on the Prairie* are a recent selections. A Christmas tradition is the annual production of the Nutcracker Suite. A private reception area is available for birthday parties and family get-togethers.

Touchstone Theater   *(610) 867-1689*

321 East Fourth Street   *e-mail: touchstone@nni.com*
Bethlehem, PA 18015   🎂 ♔♔♔ ⬧ ♞

Looking for something to do with your child this Saturday? Check out the Saturday's Child program offered by Touchstone Theater. Saturday's Child is available to parents on, when else?, Saturday. This program is offered from September through June, 11 a.m. to 2 p.m. Touchstone has a full schedule of children's theater offerings. Call for a current schedule of events.

• • •

The Art and Cultural Councils have a vast amount of information regarding other cultural activities in the area. Memberships are available and offer the benefit of current information and discounts to some events. Refer to Chapter 8 for information on regional Art and Cultural Councils.

Your family will have a memorable trip whitewater rafting on the Lehigh River. Photo courtesy Pocono Mountains Vacation Bureau, Inc.

CHAPTER
12

SPORTS

• •

Kids love to be active and the Pocono region is packed with indoor and outdoor sporting activities that are sure to please any youngster. This chapter offers information on a variety of opportunities for the active family to enjoy.

BICYCLING

Did you know that Wayne County has more dirt roads than anywhere in the northeast? Amazing! The Pocono region is a great place to bike. The area's state parks and the Delaware Water Gap Recreation Area offer numerous bike paths for little peddlers and their families. Refer to Chapter 10 and contact the parks that indicate bike trails as an amenity, then call the park for specific information and to request a map. If you speak with the staff at a bike rental shop, ask them to advise you on places to bike in the area. The outfitters listed here do not offer baby seat rental or children's bikes with training wheels, although most shops have small frame bikes available to fit the young adult rider.

Jim Thorpe River Adventures

1 Adventure Lane
Jim Thorpe, PA 18229

(717) 325-2570
(717) 325-4960
www.jtraft.com

Description: Situated directly across from a 25-mile bike route, Jim Thorpe River Adventures offers a full line of bikes, helmets, and accessories. The bike route is on a slight incline to make the trip enjoyable for both the beginner and expert.

Hours: Year-round: Monday through Friday, 8 a.m. to 7 p.m.; Saturday and Sunday, 8 a.m. to 5 p.m.
Cost: $5 per hour or $25 per day (includes helmet).

Lehigh Valley Velodrome   *(610) 967-7587*

217 Main Street (business office)
Emmaus, PA 18049-2702
Routes 100 and 222 (physical location)
Trexlertown, PA   ⑧ ♿

Description: When the Lehigh Valley Velodrome is not being used for U.S. Olympic Team Cycling Trials or fast-paced bicycle racing events, the public is welcome to use this tremendous facility. The Velodrome offers community programs and public time on the track. Call first to find out the schedule, then grab your bike and helmet for some free-wheeling fun.
Hours: Vary with season.
Cost: Free.

The Loft   *(717) 629-2627*

RR #1, Box 367
Camelback Road/Sullivan Trail
Tannersville, PA 18372

Description: Mountain bike rental is available for cyclists to bike on roads near Camelback Mountain, in nearby state parks, or in Jacobsburg State Park located thirty minutes south of the Poconos. The bikes available are limited and rented on a first-come, first-served basis. Bike racks are also available to rent.
Hours: May through October: Monday through Friday, 9 a.m. to 7 p.m.; Saturday and Sunday, 9 a.m. to 6 p.m.
Cost: $25 per day and $15 for a half day.

Northeast Sports   *(717) 253-1145*

107 8th Street
Honesdale, PA 18431

Description: Are you looking for an all-day adventure or a guided overnight expedition? Northeast Sports can offer you both. Bike and helmet rental, bike rack rental, and delivery to the site can be arranged. The staff will customize trail maps for your level.

Northeast Sports has an Adventure Club that offers group mountain bike activities during the summer.

Hours: Monday through Thursday, 9 a.m. to 6 p.m.; Friday, 9 a.m. to 8 p.m.; Saturday, 9 a.m. to 5 p.m.; Sunday, hours vary with season, so call first.

Cost: Monday through Thursday, $30 a day; Friday through Sunday and holidays, $35 a day.

Peck's Pond Bike Rentals   *(717) 775-7237*

Star Route 485
Pecks Pond, PA 18328

Description: Rent a bike, a boat, or both! Your youngest rider must be at least 16 years old. Riders are provided with maps of the area. Peck's Pond Store has a combination bike and canoe rental at a special price.

Hours: Year-round; Sunday through Saturday, 7 a.m. to 7 p.m.

Cost: Bike rental is $19 for 10 hours or $10 for 5 hours. A special canoe/bike combo is $25.

Peterson Ski and Cycle   *(717) 646-9223*

PO Box 676, Route 115
Blakeslee, PA 18610

Description: This shop provides maps of easy access riding in the area. A multi-day rate is available. The local riding club meets every Thursday at the shop for some serious biking. The group is informal and welcomes new riders.

Hours: Monday through Wednesday and Friday through Sunday, 10 a.m. to 6 p.m.; Thursday, 10 a.m. to 5 p.m.

Cost: $6 per hour, $15 for 4 hours, or $20 for a full day.

Pocono Bicycle Tours, Inc.   *(717) 226-7303*

PO Box 114
Palmyra Professional Complex
Hawley, PA 18428

Description: Guided bicycle tours are offered throughout the Pike and Wayne County region. Half day, full day, and a special country inn overnight trek are tour options available to you and your family. The half-day trip ranges from 15 to 20 miles and the full day runs 35 to 40 miles. Bikes are available to rent or you may bring your own. The guide can select a route accommodating beginning and advanced riders. Reservations are strongly recommended. Guided group tours are available, yet no more than 10 riders per trip are permitted. The minimum age for riders is 12 years old.

Hours: Sunday through Saturday, 8:30 a.m. to 5 p.m.

Cost: A guided tour with your bike is $19 for a half day or $24 for a full day. A guided tour with a rented bike is $31 for half a day or $36 for a full day.

Pocono Whitewater Bike Tours   *(717) 325-8430*

Route 903   *www.whitewaterrafting.com*
HC-2, Box 2245   *e-mail: rafting@whitewaterrafting.com*
Jim Thorpe, PA 18229   ♦♦♦

Description: There are two self-guided tours available for the family who is up for the all-day bike hike. Select a 17- or 20-mile bike ride through the Lehigh Gorge. This four- to six-hour trip can be expanded to include picnicking, swimming, or side hikes into the beautiful state park that surrounds the riders. Reservations and deposits are required. The bike shuttle is included in the price.

Hours: Year-round: Sunday through Saturday, 8:30 a.m. to 8 p.m.

Cost: $30 for a 17-mile trip and $35 for a 20-mile trip.

Whitewater Challengers Bike Tours   *(717) 443-9532*

PO Box 8   *(800) 443-8554*
Route 940   *www.wcrafting.com*
White Haven, PA 18661   *e-mail: wcrafting@microserve.net*
                                                   ♦♦♦

Description: For this trip, you'll choose among the 60 miles of suitable bike paths between White Haven and Jim Thorpe, including trails within Lehigh Gorge State Park. Shuttle service is available. The minimum age for bike rental is 10 years old. A four-hour tour is the suggested minimum.

Hours: March through October: Sunday through Saturday, 8 a.m. to 6 p.m.

Cost: $25 per day without shuttle, $35 per day with shuttle, or $5 per hour (4 hour minimum).

Boating, Canoeing, and Rafting

Whatever floats your boat, you'll find it in the Poconos. The Poconos is home to a maze of waterways. The main ones offer beauty as well as the adventure of boating, canoeing, tubing, or rafting. The outfitters listed here provide trips on the Delaware River, the Lehigh River, and the Lackawaxen River. It is suggested that you call in advance for reservations as well as for the information on group and special discounts. All prices generally include the water craft, life vests, paddles, and parking for your vehicle. In most cases the prices will also include transportation to and from the river, but be sure to ask when firming up plans. River maps and a brief orientation of water safety are common with most outfitters. The age and swimming ability of each child should be taken into consideration when traveling on the river. Please discuss this with your outfitter prior to your trip. If you plan on bringing snacks or lunch, please remember that alcoholic beverages and glass are not allowed. You must also take all your garbage with you, so keep this in mind when packing for the expedition.

Delaware River

Adventure Sports

(800) 487-2628

PO Box 175	*(717) 223-0505*
Route 209	*www.poconomall.com/adventuresports*
Marshalls Creek, PA 18335	*e-mail: sports@poconomall.com*

Description: With over 30 years of experience on the Delaware River, Adventure Sports has canoes and rafts available to rent. Overnight guided camping and canoe trips are also available. Groups of 10 or more require advance reservations.

Hours: April through October: Monday through Friday, 9 a.m. to 6 p.m.; Saturday and Sunday, 8 a.m. to 6 p.m.

Cost: $23 per person for rafts (4 person minimum); $23 per person for canoes (2 person minimum).

Chamberlain Canoes

(717) 421-0180

PO Box 155
Minisink Acres
Minisink Hills, PA 18341

(800) 422-6631

Description: Tubing, canoeing, and rafting trips are available. Double tubes are available for parents who would like to team up with one of the kids. Overnight camping and canoeing trips can also be arranged. The staff will customize the trip to suit your family's needs. Trips range from 4 miles up to 20 miles for a multi-day excursion.

Hours: Monday through Friday, 9 a.m. to 6 p.m.; Saturday, Sunday, and holidays, 8 p.m. to 6 p.m.

Cost: $13 per person for tubing, $23 per person for rafting or canoeing.

Indian Head Canoe and Raft Trips

(800) 874-BOAT

1065 Delaware Drive
Matamoras, PA 18336

www.indianheadcanoes.com
e-mail: from web site

Description: Enjoy self-guided trips in rafts, canoes, or double kayaks. Raft trips range from 7 to 9 miles. Canoe and kayak trips run 14 to 18 miles. Minimum weight of 30 pounds is required for children to participate. To extend your adventure, families and large groups may take advantage of the on-site bunkhouse. If your family is able to make the river trip on the weekend, Indian Head hosts an all-you-can-eat BBQ.

Hours: Monday through Friday, 9 a.m. to 6 p.m.; Saturday and Sunday, 8 a.m. to 6 p.m.

Cost:: Family rates: Monday through Friday, $23 a person (2 person minimum); Saturday and Sunday, $25 a person (3 person minimum); children 12 and under are free.

Pennsylvania Trivia

The lowest point in the state is the
Delaware River.

Kittatinny Canoes

(800) FLOAT-KC

PA Hwy. 739 S.
Dingmans Ferry, PA 18328

(800) 356-2852
www.kittatinny.com
e-mail: from web site

Description: Canoeing, rafting, tubing, and kayaking are all available. Trips range from 2 to 8 miles. Inquire about the Learn to Kayak and Canoe Days. Call in advance for reservations, especially on weekends.

Hours: Monday through Friday, 9 a.m. to 5 p.m.; Saturday and Sunday, 8 a.m. to 5 p.m.

Cost: Canoes and rafts are $23 per person on weekdays and $26 per person on weekends. Tubing is $14 per person. Kayaks are $29 per person.

Pack Shack Adventures, Inc.

(717) 424-8533

88 Broad Street
PO Box 127
Delaware Water Gap, PA 18327

(800) 424-0955

Description: Canoeing, kayaking, tubing, and rafting are available. Day and overnight trips on the Delaware River should also be considered. Reservation discounts are available. The outfitter will take care of everything for you and your family to have a great day on the river.

Hours: Monday through Friday, 9 a.m. to 6 p.m.; Saturday and Sunday, 8 a.m. to 6 p.m.

Cost: Canoeing and rafting is $25 for adults, $10 for children ages 13 to 17, and $5 for children ages 2 to 12. Tubing is $16 for adults, $10 for children ages 13 to 17, and $5 for children ages 2 to 12. Kayaking is $37 for adults; no children allowed.

Peck's Pond Boat Rental

(717) 775-7237

Star Route Box 485
Pecks Pond, PA 18328

Description: Boats are available for fishing or simply to paddle around and relax on the lakes in the area. Transportation of boats to lakes is available for a fee. The rental of a boat includes life vests, boat cushions, and paddles.

Hours: Sunday through Saturday, 7 a.m. to 7 p.m.
Cost: Rowboats are $7 an hour or $17 a day; motorboats are $37 a
day; and transportation is $25.

Shawnee Canoe Trips   *(717) 421-1500, ext. 1120*

PO Box 67
River Road
Shawnee on Delaware, PA 18356

Description: Don't let the name fool you. In addition to canoe rides,
Shawnee Canoes provides rafting and tubing trips on the Delaware River. Trips leave on the hour from Shawnee Inn. Canoe
trips include your choice of a 13-mile or an overnight excursion. Tubing and rafting trips are 3-mile floats and last about
three hours. Contact the outfitter for reservations.
Hours: Memorial Day through Labor Day: 9 a.m. to 5 p.m.
Cost: A canoe is $22 midweek and $24 on weekends. Rafting and
tubing is $14 midweek and $16 on weekends.

Lackawaxen River

Scotty's Whitewater Rafting   *(717) 226-3551*

RD #1, Box 646
Hawley, PA 18428   ♦♦♦

Description: Lackawaxen is a Native American term meaning "body
of slow and fast moving water." Venture out to see how true
this is. The river is located just 5 miles from Lake Wallenpaupak.
There are dam releases throughout the week that raise the water level 2 to 3 feet. Guided and self-guided tours are available
for rafting. The whitewater rafting trip is 12½ miles and lasts
two to three hours depending on the water level. Also offered is
an 8-mile tubing trip. The rapids start small but get bigger and
last longer as you head down the river—23 rapids in all. If the
water level is low in the Lackawaxen, a Delaware River trip is
also available.
Hours: March through October: Sunday through Saturday, 9 a.m. to
5 p.m.
Cost: Rafting: a deposit is required, and special family rates are available. At least two people in the group must be over 21 years of

age. $24 per person for a group of four. Add $40 for a guided rafting trip. Tubing is $22 per person for adults and requires a $5 deposit per tube.

Lehigh River

Jim Thorpe River Adventures (717) 325-2570

1 Adventure Lane   *www.wtraft.com*
Jim Thorpe, PA 18229

Description: In the early spring and fall your family can experience Class 4 rapids on the Lehigh River. This whitewater rafting trip runs about 16 miles and last between four and six hours. In the summer, enjoy a leisurely 8-mile float down this beautiful river, taking approximately three to four hours. The minimum age for rafting is 10 years old, while the youngest tuber can be 5 years of age.

Hours: March through October: Sunday to Saturday, 9 a.m. to 6 p.m.

Cost: Rafting is $46 for per adult or child. Tubing is $28 per adult and $20 per child.

Pocono Whitewater Adventures (800) WHITEWATER

HC-2, Box 2245   *(717) 839-2265*
Route 903   *www/whitewaterrafting.com*
Jim Thorpe, PA 18229   *e-mail: from web site*

Description: Guided rafting and tubing trips on the Lehigh River carry you through the Lehigh Gorge to the outskirts of the charming village of Jim Thorpe. Tours can last from five hours for a float trip to a seven to eight hour whitewater rafting trip. Whitewater rafting is offered in the spring and fall, while tubing is only available in the summer months of late June, July, August, and early September.

Hours: March through October: Sunday through Saturday, 8:30 a.m. to 8 p.m.

Cost: Rafting is $49 for adults and children ages 10 to 16. Tubing is $33 for adults and $19.95 for children ages 5 to 16.

Whitewater Challengers, Inc.

(717) 443-9532

PO Box 8
Route 940
White Haven, PA 18661

(800) 443-8554
www.wcrafting.com
e-mail: wcrafting@microserve.net
†††

Description: Offering more than river trips, this outfitter is well-suited to provide your family with a fun day on the river. The fast water runs March through mid-June, then again in September and October for some great rafting fun. The minimum age accepted on whitewater rafting trips is 10 years old. For tubing, which starts at the end of June and runs through August, the minimum age is 5 years old. If your family is inclined, Whitewater Challengers offers kayak clinics and orienteering classes. Orienteering is the skill of finding your way in a wooded area with a compass. This class is gaining popularity so call ahead.

Hours: March through October: Sunday through Saturday, 8 a.m. to 6 p.m.

Cost: Rafting is $47 for adults and children (10 years old minimum). Tubing is $31 for adults and $19 for children ages 5 to 17.

Whitewater Rafting Adventures, Inc.

(800) 876-0285

PO Box 88
Route 534
Albrightsville, PA 18210

www.adventurerafting.com
e-mail: WRA@ptd.net
†††

Description: What better way to end the day on the river than with a cookout? That's what you'll get when you complete your river trip with Whitewater Rafting Adventures. Whitewater rafting is available in the spring and fall. Tubing is offered in the summer months. Family rates can be provided.

Hours: March through October: Sunday through Saturday, 8 a.m. to 8 p.m.

Cost: Rafting is $45 for adults and children (10 years old and up). Tubing is $29 for adults. A family rate is available for tubing: $19 each for two adults, and the first child (5 years old and up) is free.

Lake Wallenpaupack

Action Sports Marina
(717) 857-1976

Route 507 and Tanglewood Lodge
Lake Wallenpaupack, PA

Description: Rentals include ski and fishing boats, sailboats, canoes, and rowboats. Depending on the age of your children, there are wave runners and jet skis available as well as waterskiing instruction.

Pine Crest Boat Rentals
(717) 857-1136

Route 507
Lake Wallenpaupack, PA

Description: Here you can rent fishing boats, canoes, rowboats, and sailboats. Jet skis and waverunners are also available for the more daring.

If you're lucky, some feathered friends may join you when you row.
Photo courtesy Jim McElholm.

BOWLING

If your family members are seasoned bowlers or you're just looking for some indoor fun, the lanes listed below are worth checking out. There are no reservations required, and the public may use the lanes whenever they are not being used by the bowling leagues. All the lanes listed have junior leagues for young adults to play competitively, and some offer bumper leagues which are geared toward the preschooler. Sign-ups for winter and summer leagues are taken at the front desk. Birthday parties can be accommodated with ease at all the lanes. Reservations for parties and large groups need to be made in advance. Fees are based on a per game basis and include use of the bowling balls. Bowling shoes may be rented for an additional fee. Call for exact times and prices.

Ashley Lanes   *(610) 377-5022*

Second and South Street
Lehighton, PA 18235

   Junior League

Colonial Lanes   *(717) 421-5941*

Route 611
Stroudsburg, PA 18360

   Junior League

Cypress Lanes   *(610) 377-4570*

140 North 4th Street
Lighighton, PA 18235

   Junior League

Pocono Lanes   *(717) 595-2518*

Buck Hill Fork
Mountainhome, PA 18342

   Junior League, Bumper League

Sky Lanes   *(717) 421-7680*

100 Eagle Valley Mall
East Stroudsburg, PA 18301

   Junior Leagues, Bumper League

FISHING

In addition to fishing in the public lakes and streams, the Poconos has several private hatcheries and preserves in which to fish. Families can take advantage of a beautiful or not-so-beautiful day to enjoy the outdoors. No licenses are required to fish at any of the lakes listed below. All equipment can be rented and bait is available at the facilities. Picnic tables are provided for families to bring their own lunch and relax. No grilling is permitted.

Big Brown Fish and Pay Lake   *(717) 629-0427*

PO Box 584
Route 115
Effort, PA 18330

Description: Two ponds are stocked with trout as well as bass, bluegills, and catfish. You must keep what you catch, but you are only charged for trout and bass. There is a tackle shop on the premises as well as a small snack shop. Special family days include opening day, Mother's Day, and Father's Day.
Hours: March through November: Sunday through Saturday, 8 a.m. to 5 p.m. (7 p.m. during summer).
Cost: The entrance fee is $2 for people over the age of 12, $1.50 for senior citizens, and free for children under 12. Pole rental is $5 a pole. Trout is $4.05 a pound, and bass is $5.50 a pound.

Paradise Trout Preserve   *(717) 629-0422*

Route 191
RD #1
Cresco, PA 18326

Description: The oldest licensed fish hatchery in Pennsylvania offers excellent trout fishing on a one-acre pond as well as a self-guided tour of the on-site hatchery. There is no charge for the tour.
Hours: April through October: Sunday through Saturday, 8 a.m. to 5 p.m.
Cost: $2 per person, $3 per rod, and trout are $3.75 a pound.

HORSEBACK RIDING

Horseback riding in the Poconos is a popular family activity. The stables listed below offer riding orientation prior to the trail ride. Most stables will not take riders under 8 years of age, regardless of size. The younger set, where noted, are accommodated either with a special pony or wagon ride. Wearing helmets is encouraged but not required. Safety is a priority; therefore, the horses on trail rides are typically kept at a walk or a trot. The more experienced rider may inquire about private lessons or special trips. Physically-challenged individuals are gladly accommodated with some advance notice. Many of the stables host special-need groups year after year. Reservations are strongly suggested and required on weekends. Please arrive 15 minutes prior to your scheduled time to be properly suited to a horse. All trail rides are subject to weather.

Carson's Riding Stables, Inc.   (717) 839-9841

RD #1, Box 262   *www.poconos.org*
Cresco, PA 18326

Description: Take an ordinary day and make it special by planning a guided 3½-mile trail ride lasting one hour through 60 acres of Pocono Mountain woods. Chances are riders will see some wildlife on the path.
Hours: Year-round: Sunday through Saturday, 10 a.m. to 5 p.m. Closed Christmas Day.
Cost: $20 per hour for adults and children.

Deer Path Riding Stables, Inc.   (717) 443-7047

Route 940
White Haven, PA 18661

Description: Spend some time riding on an old dairy farm, surrounded by 5000 acres of state game land. The walk/trot trail ride will take you into the wilderness to see deer, turkey, and an occasional bear. The staff specializes in first-time riders, physically-challenged riders, and groups, including 4-H members and Scouts. Riders need to be at least 9 years old. Riders 8 and under are offered pony rides. Family specials run throughout the year and an out-of-school special in June allows you to pay by the pound of the child.
Hours: Year-round: Sunday through Saturday, 8 a.m. to 4:30 p.m.
Cost: $22 for adults, $20 for children ages 9 to 12.

Mountain Creek Riding Stables   *(717) 839-8725*

RR #1, Box 499   *www.poconos.org*
Route 940
Cresco, PA 18326

Description: A one hour, 3½-mile trail ride starts by crossing over a mountain stream and continuing into the woods to see various Pocono wildlife. All safety equipment is available, including Little Dudes (Little Dudes allow the short-legged rider a better fit in the stirrup). Riders need to be at least 7 years old or 50" tall. Riders under these requirements may enjoy a pony ride or horse-drawn wagon ride that follows the trail. The wagon ride is a perfect alternative for grandparents, too. Guides are certified in first aid and CPR. Physically-challenged riders are accommodated with advance notice. Reservations are strongly suggested.

Hours: Year-round: Sunday through Saturday, 8 a.m. to 5 p.m.

Cost: $20 for adults and children. Wagon rides are $10 for adult and $8 for children.

Shawnee Stables   *(717) 420-1763*

PO Box 400   *www.quikpage.com/W/windroser*
River Road   *e-mail: windrose@ptd.net*
Minisink Hills, PA 18341

Description: Situated in the Delaware River Valley on 75 acres of woods and fields, families can take a 45-minute trail ride. Staff will fit riders with the proper size horse. Reservations are recommended.

Hours: Year-round: Sunday through Saturday, 8 a.m. to 4:30 p.m. Closed Wednesdays in winter.

Cost: $22 for adults and children.

Pennsylvania Trivia

By the year 1890, most of the trees in the Poconos were cut down because of the logging industry. Therefore, the majority of the trees in the area are less than 100 years old.

Triple W Riding Stable, Inc.

(800) 540-2620

RR #2, Box 1540
Honesdale, PA 18431

(717) 226-2620

Description: Trail rides may be taken for a one-hour minimum over different types of terrain. At one point of the ride, the group will be poised on a mountaintop with a 25-mile view. Riders need to be at least 6 years old. Customized trail rides with lunch provided may be pre-arranged.

Hours: Year-round: Sunday through Saturday, 8 a.m. to 5 p.m.

Cost: Weekdays: $25 for one hour, $37.50 for one and a half hours, and $48 for two hours. Weekends: Add $2 to the weekday rates.

MINIATURE GOLF

Miniature Golf is seasonal fun. Most courses open in March or April and close when the weather gets cold. All the miniature golf courses offer birthday party and group rates. Wheelchair and stroller accessibility is available as well. Miniature golf courses have 18 holes with a 19th hole that gives the player an opportunity to win a free game. At the end of the course, why not treat the family to some ice cream? (Most facilities have on-site ice cream parlors.) Hours given are during the prime summer season. Prior to Memorial Day and post-Labor Day the hours change considerably. Please call to avoid disappointment.

940 Golf N' Fun Family Play Park

(717) 646-0700

Route 940
Pocono Lake, PA 18347

Description: Ice cream parlor.

Hours: May through September: Sunday through Saturday, 10 a.m. to 11 p.m.

Cost: $4.25 for adults and youths, $3 for children ages 3 to 6, and free for children under 3.

Casino Theater
(717) 839-7831

Route 611, Main Street
Mount Pocono, PA 18344

Description: Ice cream parlor and movie theater.
Hours: March through November: Sunday through Saturday, 11 a.m.
to 11 p.m.
Cost: $3 for adults and youth (over 48"), $2 for children (under 48").

Eagle Valley Miniature Golf
(717) 476-4630

727 North Courtland Street
East Stroudsburg, PA 18301

Description: Ice cream parlor and pizza place nearby.
Hours: Memorial Day through Labor Day: Sunday through Saturday, 12 noon to 10 p.m.
Cost: $4.75 for adults, $3.75 for children ages 4 to 12, and free for
children 3 and under. Family Special on weekdays: 4 to 6 players are $15 per round of golf.

Fun and Games
(717) 253-9111

Plaza Center Mall
Honesdale, PA 18431

Description: Refer to Chapter 10.

Golf Plus Park
(717) 689-4996

RD #1, Golf Park Drive
Lake Ariel, PA 18436

Description: Refer to Chapter 10.

King of Swing Miniature Golf
(717) 424-9045

River Road
Minisink Hills, PA 18341

Description: Ice cream parlor, hot dogs, and batting cages, too!
Hours: April through October: Sunday to Saturday, 10 a.m. to
10 p.m.
Cost: $4 for adults, $3 for children ages 6 to 12, and free for children
5 and under.

Mystic Pines Miniature Golf — *(717) 223-9227*

Route 209
Marshalls Creek, PA 18335

Description: Ice cream parlor.
Hours: April through November: Sunday through Saturday, 10 a.m. to 12 midnight.
Cost: $5 for adults, $4 for children ages 12 and under.

Rocky Road Miniature Golf — *(717) 223-1993*

Liberty Square
Route 209
Marshalls Creek, PA 18335

Description: No concessions available.
Hours: Memorial Day through Labor Day: Monday through Thursday, 2 p.m. to 9 p.m.; Friday, 2 p.m. to 11 p.m.; Saturday and Sunday, 12 noon to 10 p.m.
Cost: $4.50 for adults, $3.50 for children ages 13 and under.

SKIING
Cross-Country Skiing

As long as Mother Nature cooperates, cross-country skiing lovers will be able to enjoy several area courses. If you have your own equipment, rentals are not an issue and your choice of locations expand. All of the national and state parks in the Pocono region (*see* Chapter 10) provide trails for cross-country skiing. If you are trying this type of skiing for the first time, it would be wise to dress in layers. You get quite a workout with this type of skiing, and to stay comfortable, you may need to shed some layers as you go. It is also advised that you call in advance for snow conditions and availability of equipment.

Cross-Country Skiing Hot Line

(provides Pocono Mountain ski conditions) *(717) 421-5565*

Big Boulder/Jack Frost   (717) 722-0100

PO Box 702   *Snow Report: (717) 722-0100*
Blakeslee, PA 18610

Description: The resort opens an 8-mile fitness trail to all who are interested in cross-country skiing. Equipment is available for rental.
Hours: Winter months: trail available from dawn to dusk. Rental shop: Sunday through Saturday, 8 a.m. to 4 p.m.
Cost: The trail fee is $10 a day. Trail fee and rental is $42 a day.

Cliff Park Inn   (800) 225-6535

Cliff Park Road   *(717) 296-6491*
Milford, PA 18337   *www.cliffparkinn.com*
                               e-mail: cpi@warwick.net

Description: Guests of Cliff Park Inn as well as the public may enjoy the golf course for an initiation to cross-country skiing. If you are experienced, you may want to try the seven miles of marked trails throughout the 600 acres of adjacent woods. At the end of your trek, warm up (or cool down) with refreshments in the restaurant at Cliff Park Inn. Children's rental equipment is limited. It will be assigned on a first-come, first-served basis. Get there early.
Hours: Daily, 9 a.m. to 4 p.m.
Cost: No trail fee; rentals are $10 per person per day.

Evergreen Park Cross-Country Skiing   (717) 421-7721

Route 447
Analomink, PA 18320

Description: Take an easy glide through natural snow on the golf course at Evergreen Park. Throughout the winter months this golf course offers cross-country skiing to the public.
Hours: Winter months: dawn to dusk. Rentals: Sunday through Saturday, 8 a.m. to 5 p.m.
Cost: Call for prices.

Fernwood Resort

(800) 233-8103

Route 209
Bushkill, PA 18324

Snow Report: (717) 588-9500

Description: The golf course at this family-oriented resort is open for cross-country skiing when the snow is on the ground. Full equipment rental is available. A stop at this resort allows you to not only enjoy the cross-country skiing, but the many other amenities. Refer to Chapter 1 for more information.

Hours: Winter months: trail, dawn to dusk. Rental shop: call ahead for hours.

Cost: No trail fee; rentals are $25 a day.

Split Rock Lodge

(717) 722-9111, ext. 607

Box 547A
Lake Harmony, PA 18624

Snow Report: (717) 722-9111, ext. 606

Description: At the rear of the resort, an area is available for families who would like to cross-country ski. As always, call ahead for snow conditions. Rental of equipment is available on-site.

Hours: Winter months: trail, dawn to dusk. Rental shop: 9:30 a.m. to 4 p.m.

Cost: Trail and rental are $13 for adults and $9 for children.

Downhill Skiing

The Pocono Mountains are home to the majority of ski slopes in Pennsylvania. When the weather gets cold, the ski resorts get hot. Their popularity is due to easy accessibility and great conditions. Keep in mind that lift ticket costs are based on time of day as well as day of the week. Midweek passes are less expensive than weekend tickets. Each mountain has various options and special deals. Many of the area inns, hotels, and resorts have special ski-and-stay discount packages. In addition to downhill skiing, most of the mountains provide snow tubing and snowboarding parks. Even if you're not a skier you can still enjoy the après-ski atmosphere. All the mountains sponsor some fantastic events and celebrations throughout the season for everyone to enjoy. One important number to keep handy is the Pocono Ski Hot Line ((717) 421-5565). This number will give you up-to-date information on all the ski resorts in the region.

Alpine Mountain Ski Area   *(717) 595-2150*

Route 447   *Snow Report: (717) 595-2150*
PO Box 309   *www.dawnserver.com/alpine*
Analomink, PA 18320

Facilities: 18 trails, 3 lifts, 500 ft. vertical drop
Amenities: On-site rentals, snowboard rentals, lodge available, ski school
Other activities: Snow tubing, snowboarding

Big Boulder Ski Area   *(717) 722-0100*

PO Box 702   *Snow Report: (717) 722-0100*
Blakeslee, PA 18610   *www.big2resorts.com*

Facilities: 14 trails, 7 lifts, 475 ft. vertical drop
Amenities: On-site rentals, snowboard rentals, lodge available, ski school
Other activities: Snow tubing (3 hills, 4 tows), snowboarding

Blue Mountain Ski Area   *(610) 826-7700*

PO Box 216   *Snow Report: (800) 235-2226*
Palmerton, PA 18071   *www/aninews.com/bluemountain*

Facilities: 19 trails, 7 lifts, 1082 ft. vertical drop
Amenities: On-site rentals, lodge available, ski school
Other activities: Snow tubing (5 hills, 2 tows)

Camelback Ski Area   *(717) 629-1661*

PO Box 168   *silo.com/poconos/camelback/home.htm*
Snow Report: (800) 233-8100   *e-mail: Camelback@silo.com*

Facilities: 32 trails (22 at night), 12 lifts, 800 ft. vertical drop
Amenities: On-site rentals, snowboard rentals, lodge available, ski
    school, snowboard park
Other activities: Snow tubing (6 hills, 2 tows), snowboarding

Pennsylvania Trivia

*Snow making for ski slopes was first introduced at
Big Boulder Ski Area in Carbon County.*

Fernwood Resort
(717) 588-9500

Route 209
Bushkill, PA 18324

Facilities: 2 trails, 1 lift, 225 ft. vertical drop
Amenities: On-site rentals, snowboard rentals, lodge available, ski
  school
Other activities: Snowboarding

Jack Frost Mountain
(717) 443-8425

PO Box 703　　　　　　　　　　Snow Report: (717) 443-8425
Blakeslee, PA 18610

Facilities: 21 trails, 7 lifts, 600 ft. vertical drop
Amenities: On-site rentals, snowboard rentals, lodge available, ski
  school
Other activities: Snow tubing, snowboarding

Montage Mountain Skiing
(717) 969-7669

PO Box 3539　　　　　　　　　　　　　　*Snow Report*
(800) 468-7669
Scranton, PA 18505

Facilities: 21 trails, 7 lifts, 1000 ft. vertical drop
Amenities: On-site rentals, snowboard rentals, lodge available, ski
  school
Other activities: Snowboarding

Mount Tone Ski Area
(800) 747-2754

PO Box 217　　　　　　　　　　　　　　(717) 798-2707
Wallerville Road
Lake Como, PA 18437

Facilities: 10 trails, 3 lifts, 450 ft. vertical drop
Amenities: On-site rentals, snowboard rentals, lodge available, ski
  school
Other activities: Snow tubing, snowboarding

Shawnee Mountain Ski Area
(717) 421-7231

PO Box 339
Hollow Road
Shawnee on Delaware, PA 18356

Snow Report: (800) 233-4218
www.shawneemt.com

Facilities: 23 trails, 10 lifts, 700 ft. vertical drop
Amenities: On-site rentals, snowboard rentals, lodge available, ski school
Other activities: Snow tubing, snowboarding

Ski Big Bear
(717) 685-1400

HC # 1, 1A353
Karl Hope Blvd.
Lackawaxen, PA 18435

Facilities: 10 trails, 1 lifts, 250 ft. vertical drop
Amenities: On-site rentals, snowboard rentals, lodge available, ski school, snowboard park
Other activities: Snow tubing, snowboarding

Split Rock Lodge
(717) 722-9111, ext. 607

PO Box 547A
Lake Harmony, PA 18624

Snow Report: (717) 722-9111, ext. 606

Facilities: 7 trails, 2 lifts, 415 ft. vertical drop
Amenities: On-site rentals, snowboard rentals, lodge available, ski school
Other activities: Snowboarding

Tanglewood Ski Area
(717) 226-9500

PO Box 257
Hawley, PA 18428

Facilities: 10 trails, 5 lifts, 415 ft. vertical drop
Amenities: On-site rentals, snowboard rentals, lodge available, ski school
Other activities: Snowboarding

ICE SKATING

Another great family sport in the winter is ice skating. The information below is given for both indoor and outdoor rinks. When Mother Nature cooperates, the area state parks (*see* Chapter 10) have some great lakes on which to enjoy an afternoon of ice skating. All you'll need is some warm clothes, ice skates, and a container of hot chocolate to have a great day.

Lackawanna Stadium on Ice   *(717) 969-2255*

Montage Mountain Road
Moosic, PA 18507

Description: By summer this outdoor rink is known as Red Barons Baseball Stadium, but when the temperatures drop, the stadium transforms into an outdoor ice-skating rink. The large professional size ice-skating rink offers lots of cool outdoor family fun. Special days to take advantage of are Cheap Skate Night and Family Night. Both provide great skating at reduced rates. Rentals are available at the rink.

Hours: December through March: Monday through Thursday, 5:30 p.m. to 9:30 p.m.; Friday, 5:30 p.m. to 12 midnight; Saturday, 10 a.m. to 10 p.m.; Sunday, 12 noon to 9 p.m.

Cost: $4 for adults, $3.50 for youths ages 15 to 20, $2.50 for junior youths ages 6 to 14, and free for children under 6. Skate rental is $2.50 a pair.

Mountain Manor Inn   *(717) 223-8098*

PO Box 1067
Marshalls Creek, PA 18335

Description: This indoor ice-skating rink, available during the winter months, is a great place to chase the cold-weather blues away. Tuesday and Thursday nights are Hockey Nights. Double-runner skates are available for the littlest of skaters.

Hours: Thanksgiving through Easter: Sunday through Saturday, 10 a.m. to 5 p.m. and 7 p.m. to 10 p.m.

Cost: $6 for adults and $4 for children 12 and under. Skate rental is $4 a pair.

Peck's Pond Store   *(717) 775-7237*

Route 402
HC 67, Box 485
Dingmans Ferry, PA 18328

Description: Outdoor skating on Peck's Pond is available when the weather cooperates. Skate rental is available at the store. Families that own their own skates may skate on this pond after paying the per person skating fee.

Hours: Hours vary depending on ice and weather condition.

Cost: The skating fee is $5 for adults and children. Call in advance for the price of rentals.

Pocono Ice-a-Rama   *(717) 421-6465*

PO Box 309
Analomink, PA 18320

Description: Enjoy ice skating as the music plays at the most established year-round ice-skating rink in the Poconos. The indoor rink provides tables for skaters to bring their own picnic or to just take a break with one of the beverages available from the on-site vending machines. Rentals and lessons are also available.

Hours: Year-round: Sunday through Saturday, 10 a.m. to 9 p.m.

Cost: Weekdays: $4.75 for adults and $4.25 for children ages 10 and under. Weekends: $5.75 for adults and $4.75 for children ages 10 and under. Skate rentals are $3.75 a pair.

Pennsylvania Trivia

Jim Thorpe in Carbon County is also known as the "Switzerland of America."

ROLLER SKATING, IN-LINE SKATING, AND SKATEBOARDING

The all-season activity of roller skating has taken many turns over the recent years. It has expanded from just roller skating to in-line skating and skateboarding. These variations on the skating theme are lots of fun and great exercise. Roller rinks are great places to pass a rainy afternoon, and many of them offer special skating programs in addition to general skating. Rentals are available on-site at an additional charge. So if you're looking for some free-wheeling fun, there's lots to choose from in the Poconos.

Big Wheel Family Skating Center   *(717) 424-5499*

3226 North 5th Street
Route 191
East Stroudsburg, PA 18301

Description: Located just north of Stroudsburg, Big Wheel has provided roller skating fun for many years. One of the all-time favorite programs is Trike, Trot, and Roll for preschoolers and parents. The rink is open for all toddler vehicles, so preschoolers and their parents may socialize and learn to skate. Admission fee includes kiddie skates. Weekly family nights and open skating times give parents and their children lots of time to learn to skate and have fun together. A full-service snack bar is on the premises for your enjoyment.

Hours: Trike, Trot, and Roll: September through June: Wednesday, 10 a.m. to 12 noon. The hours change every season. Call ahead for the schedule of family nights and open-skating times.

Cost: Trike, Trot, and Roll: $3.50 per child including skate rental. Family night and open skate: depending on day of the week, $4.50 to $6.50, including skate rental.

Big Wheel North   *(717) 491-1117*

PO Box 132
Route 209
Matamoras, PA 18336

Description: Big Wheel North is operated by the same owners of the Big Wheel in Stroudsburg. The programs are similar. Trike, Trot, and Roll is available as well as family nights and open skating. If you live or are visiting the northern tier of the Poconos, Big Wheel North is worth visiting.

Hours: Trike, Trot, and Roll: September through June: Tuesdays, 10 a.m. to 12 noon. The hours change every season so call ahead for the schedule of family nights and open-skating times.

Cost: Trike, Trot, and Roll: $3 per child including skate rental. Family night and open skate: depending on the day of the week, $4 to $6, including skate rental.

LeRose's Roller Skating Rink   *(610) 377-1859*

Route 209
Lehighton, PA 18235

Description: Located in the western portion of the Pocono area is LeRose's Roller Skating Rink. This large indoor rink offers a full line of rentals for both roller skating and in-line skating. Call in advance for times because hours change with the season.

Hours: Hours vary depending on season. Call in advance for hours.

Cost: $3.50 for adults and children, $1 for skate rental, and $2 for in-line skate rental.

Shawnee Roller Skating Rink   *(717) 421-2844*

River Road
Shawnee on Delaware, PA 18356

Description: The Shawnee Roller Rink is a small old-fashioned roller rink. Despite the size, it's packed with fun. Skate to music or play at the arcade. Snacks are available.

Hours: Monday, Tuesday, and Friday, 7:30 p.m. to 10 p.m.; Thursday, 4 p.m. to 6:30 p.m. and 7:30 p.m. to 10 p.m.; Saturday and Sunday, 2 p.m. to 4:30 p.m. and 7:30 p.m. to 10 p.m. Closed Wednesday.

Cost: Admission and rentals is $5 for adults and children. Admission alone (if you bring your own skates) is $3 for adults and children.

Pennsylvania Trivia

The motto for the Commonwealth of Pennsylvania is "Virtue, Liberty, and Independence."

The Starting Gate   (717) 223-6215

Route 209   *www.gmrcreation.com/startingGate*
Marshalls Creek, PA   *e-mail: from web site*

Description: Prior experience is necessary for this in-line skating and board park, which includes a ramp and a small course. Rentals of all equipment and pads are offered on-site, and individuals with equipment are welcome to use the park.

Hours: Sunday through Saturday, 10 a.m. to 6:30 p.m.

Cost: $7 for adults and children. Rentals: skates, skateboards, and pads are $10; pads only are $1 per pad.

Wheels In-line Skate and Board Park   (800) 468-2442

Jack Frost Mountain
PO Box 703
Route 940
Blakeslee, PA 18610

Description: Weather permitting, Wheels provides a family fun loop for easy group skating in an outdoor wooded setting. There are two freestyle areas available, so you can pick the one that suits you. Rentals are also available on-site.

Hours: Spring through fall: Sunday through Saturday, 9 a.m. to 5 p.m.

Cost: $7 for a half day and $10 for a full day. Rentals are $10 for skates and gear.

SPECTATOR SPORTS

A certain energy is derived from going to a live sporting event. While you are in the Poconos, why not check out some of what the area sport scene has to offer. Keep an eye on the local paper for the schedule of high school and college sports.

Autoracing

Nazareth Raceway   (888) 629-RACE

PO Box F
Nazareth, PA 18064

Description: April, May, and June are when the three major races take place at the Nazareth Speedway. The PPG Indy Cart Race and NASCAR series fill the stands for an evening of excitement.

Hours: Call for dates and times.
Cost: Varies with race. Contact box office in advance.

Pocono Raceway   *(800) RACEWAY*

PO Box 500   *(717) 646-2300*
Long Pond, PA 18334

Description: June and July are when Pocono Raceway is home to
two major NASCAR races. Come out for lots of fun for the whole
family.
Hours: Call for dates and times.
Cost: Varies with race. Call box office in advance

Enjoy a day at the Pocono Valley Raceway. Photo courtesy Pocono
Mountains Vacation Bureau, Inc.

Other Spectator Sports

East Stroudsburg University   *Warrior Hot Line: (717) 422-3000*

200 Prospect Street
East Stroudsburg, PA 18301

Description: If you are visiting or live in the area and enjoy a good college football, soccer, or basketball game, East Stroudsburg University has all the sports. Call the Warrior Hot Line for the latest sports schedule, which includes dates, times, and admission fees (if applicable).

Lackawanna County Stadium   *(717) 969-2255*

235 Montage Mountain Road   *www.redbarons.com*
Moosic, PA 18507   *e-mail: from web site*
                                             ⛲ 👪 ♿

Description: The 10,800-seat stadium is home to the Red Barons Minor League Baseball team. Summer evenings are filled with the thrill of the all-American baseball game. Promotional events are commonplace with bat night or other give aways for the fans. Call the box office for a season schedule. It'll be a great night out. Consider getting there a little early and tailgating or eating at the field-side restaurant.

Hours: Box office: Monday through Friday, 9 a.m. to 5 p.m.; Saturday, 10 a.m. to 4 p.m.

Cost: $6.50 for lower box, $4.50 for upper reserved, and $4 for bleachers.

Lehigh Valley Velodrome   *(610) 967-7587*

Routes 100 and 222
Trexlertown, PA   👪 ♿

Description: If cycling is your thing, you will enjoy a trip to the Lehigh Valley Velodrome. Every Friday night during the summer, the Velodrome sets the stage for high-speed competitive cycling events. A trip here will offer a chance to see international as well as domestic cycling celebrities race. In the summer of 1996, the Velodrome was host to the Olympic Cycling Trials. At the conclusion of each Friday night race, the infield is open for fans to meet with the cyclists and have an opportunity

Enjoy the fast-paced thrill of bicycle racing at the Lehigh Valley Velodrome. Photo courtesy Joe Marcus.

for photos or autographs. Refer to the biking section of this chapter to learn about public time on the track.

Hours: June through August: Friday, gates open at 6:30 p.m. and racing starts at 7:30 p.m.

Cost: Finish-line seating: $7 for adults, and $5 for senior citizens and children (12 and under). General admission: $6 for adults, and $4 for senior citizens and children (12 and under).

Pocono Downs *(717) 825-6681*

1280 Route 315
Wilkes-Barre, PA 18702

Description: Horse racing for the whole family is available at Pocono Downs Raceway. During the season, April through November, horses race live three or four times a week. Throughout the summer season, the raceway hosts various family events and festivals.

Hours: Sunday through Saturday, 12 noon to 11 p.m. Post time is 7:45 p.m.

Cost: $2.50 for adults, and free for children under 18.

Swimming

There are many, many pools in the Pocono region. If you live in the area with your family, you may have a membership at one of the public or private facilities. If you are a visitor, you may have a pool where you are staying. If neither of these situations is the case, try visiting one of the public indoor and outdoor pools listed below. If you choose to go to one of these, you will be charged per person for each visit. Some of the pools offer memberships. All pools provide lessons for young polliwogs and some have swim teams. Please give the one that interests you a call for the scoop. You may also want to inquire about birthday party facilities.

Outdoor Pools

Big Wheel Oasis
(717) 421-3347

Stroudsburg, PA

Dansbury Park Pool
(717) 421-6591

East Stroudsburg, PA

Delaware Water Gap Pool
(717) 476-0331

Delaware Water Gap, PA

Stroudsburg Pool
(717) 421-5444

Stroudsburg, PA

Indoor Pool

Pocono Family YMCA
(717) 421-2525

809 Main Street
Stroudsburg, PA 18360

Description: The YMCA hosts an open swim. This pool time is open to members and nonmembers alike. Children under 12 must be with an adult.

Hours: Tuesday, Thursday, and Friday, 3:30 p.m. to 4:30 p.m. and 6:30 p.m. to 8 p.m.; Saturday and Sunday, 1:30 p.m. to 4 p.m.

Cost: Depends on membership status. Stop at desk to inquire.

Swimming Programs

The need for a child to know how to swim is imperative, especially when considering many of the activities in this chapter. Starting them young is a great way to encourage and teach this life skill. The programs listed below are swimming programs that parent and child take together. It's a great way to spend some special time with one another.

Pocono Family YMCA
(717) 421-2525

809 Main Street
Stroudsburg, PA 18360

Description: The YMCA is home to many programs for children, yet several programs in particular are structured to include parent and child. "1, 2 and You" is a tumbling and swimming class. Toddlers 1 and 2 years of age spend 30 minutes learning forward rolls and obstacle-course maneuvers and the next half hour learning the basics of swimming. "Skippers" is a swimming-only program. Depending on the age of the child, there are different groups: Shrimps (6 to 12 months), Kippers (1 to 2 years), and Perch (2 to 3 years). In each session, the child is taught to swim through water play with the parent.

Hours: Vary depending on which class. Call to the YMCA to request a full brochure.

Cost: Varies depending on month and membership status.

Pennsylvania Trivia

The building housing the Pocono Indian Museum was once a stop on the Underground Railroad.

"Inside Out," an exhibit at the Crayola Factory, has glass walls meant to *be colored on from both sides.* Photo provided by, and reproduced with permission of, Binney & Smith, maker of Crayola products.

CHAPTER
13

TOURS

• •

Whether you are visiting the Poconos or have been a long-time resident, a tour is always entertaining and a sure way to acquaint yourself with the area and the people. Tours are usually fun for groups of all sizes and ages. In addition to being entertaining, tours are interactive and tend to fuel a child's imagination. Depending on the adventure selected, tours can also offer a broad but insightful view of career options for children.

Tours are a great activity to do with other families or another small group. Plan ahead for your excursion, because most tours need advance notice of your arrival.

AIR

Moyer Aviation, Inc.   *(717) 839-7161*

Pocono Mountain Municipal Airport
Route 611
Mount Pocono, PA 18344   ♿

Description: Moyer Aviation offers several types of air tours. If you choose the 30-minute tour your family gets to see either the Lake Wallenpaupack or Beltzville Lake area. Air tours are also available to the Delaware Water Gap or Lake Harmony area for a duration of 25 minutes each. There is also a short tour available to view the Mount Pocono area which lasts about 10 minutes. Individuals with special needs, depending upon his or her limitations, are accommodated on tours. Call in advance to arrange seating.

Hours: Year-round: 8 a.m. to dark (weather permitting).

Cost: A 30-minute tour of Lake Wallenpaupack or Beltzville Lake area is $32 per person for adults and youths; children under 6 are half price with at least two full-price paying passengers. A 25-minute tour of Delaware Water Gap or Lake Harmony area is $25 per person for adults and youths. A short tour of the Mount Pocono area is $15 per person for adults and youths; children under 6 are half price with at least two full-price paying passengers.

Sparta Aviation   *(717) 421-8900*

Stroudsburg Pocono Airport
108 Airstrip Road
East Stroudsburg, PA 18301   ⅃

Description: Enjoy a 30-minute flight around the Delaware Water Gap. The tour will take you through the Gap, along the ridge, and back along the river. This is a beautiful trip any time of year. Longer tours may be arranged to view the Gap more extensively, or you can customize the tour with your pilot. If your family or group is interested in a charter flight out of the area, Sparta Aviation will be able to handle this, too.

Hours: Year-round: 8 a.m. to dark.

Cost: A 30-minute flight is $55 for adults and children, for up to three people. A one-hour flight is $100 for up to three people.

BOAT

Canal Boat Rides   *(610) 250-6700*

Hugh Moore Park
200 South Delaware Drive (Route 611)
PO Box 877
Easton, PA 18042

Description: Step back into the early 1900s when canal boats were used for transportation along the Delaware and Lehigh Rivers. This mule-drawn canal ride will take you on a section of the Lehigh Canal. Admission to the canal museum, located in Easton, is included with the ride ticket (*see* Chapter 8).

Hours: Day after Memorial Day through the day before Labor Day:

trip departs Wednesday through Saturday at 11 a.m., 1 p.m., 2:30 p.m., and 4 p.m.; and on Sunday at 1 p.m., 2:30 p.m., and 4 p.m.. Call for off-season hours.

Cost: $5 for adults, $4.50 for senior citizens over 64, $3 for children ages 3 to 15, and free for children 3 and under.

Spirit of Paupack Scenic Boat Tours   *(717) 226-6266*

Route 507 and Route 6
Hawley, PA 18428   ♦♦♦ ⟨

Description: All aboard the Spirit of Paupack for an enjoyable one-hour sightseeing cruise, dinner cruise, or sunset cruise! Families are welcome on all, and reservations are a must.

Hours: Sightseeing Cruise: Tuesday through Saturday, trip departs at 1 p.m. and 3 p.m. Sunset Cruise: Thursday, trip departs at 7 p.m. Dinner Cruise: Wednesday, Friday, and Saturday, trip departs at 7 p.m.

Cost: *Sightseeing Cruise:* $5 for adults, and $2 for children ages 4 to 12. *Sunset Cruise:* $8.50 for adults, and $4 for children ages 4 to 12. *Dinner Cruise:* $29.50 for adults, $19.50 for children 4 to 2, and free for children 3 and under.

Wallenpaupack Scenic Boat Tour   *(717) 226-6211*

RT 6
Hawley, PA 18428   ♦♦♦ ⟨

Description: While waiting to embark on a 30-minute boat tour of the beautiful Lake Wallenpaupack, your family can enjoy the grand view from the observation dock.

Hours: May and June: weekends, 11 a.m. to 8 p.m. July through September: daily, 11 a.m. to 8 p.m.

Cost: $3.50 for adults, and $2.50 for children.

Pennsylvania Trivia

Milk is the Pennsylvania
state beverage.

BUS

...ads of Monroe County Bus Tour *(717) 424-1776*

Monroe County Historical Association
Main Street
Stroudsburg, PA 18360   ♦♦♦ ✎

Description: Once a year the Monroe County Historical Association hits the road with a day-long bus tour of the Pocono Mountains. Each year a different aspect is highlighted. A recent tour gave guests a bird's-eye view of the history of the resorts in the Pocono area.

Hours: This tour is usually hosted in the summer. Call the office for details

Cost: Members of the historical association receive a discount. Call the office for tour rates.

RAILROAD

Rail Tours, Inc.   *(717) 325-4606*

PO Box 285
Jim Thorpe, PA 18229-0285   ♦♦♦ ♿ ✎

Description: Choose from two train rides that take you back in time through the Lehigh River and Nesquehoning Valley. The longer ride wanders for 34 miles, lasting about two hours. The shorter trip is about 6 miles and takes 50 minutes. Special rides include the Fall Foliage Run, the Santa Express, and the Easter Bunny Run. No reservations taken. Admission is on a first-come, first-served basis.

Hours: Year-round: Saturdays, Sundays, and holidays.

Cost: Shorter Trip: $5 for adults, $3 for children ages 2 to 11, and free for children under 2. Longer Trip: $14 for adults, $7 for children ages 2 to 11, and free for children under 2.

Pennsylvania Trivia

The first American railroad was built in 1827 between Jim Thorpe and Summit Hill, Carbon County.

For a special adventure, hop aboard, and take a train ride through the Poconos. Photo courtesy Pocono Mountains Vacation Bureau, Inc.

Steamtown National Historic Site

(888) 693-9391

150 South Washington Avenue
Scranton, PA 18503

(717) 340-5200
♊ ♿ ✎

Description: This historic site, solely dedicated to railroad history, is home to the Steamtown Train ride. The round-trip from Scranton to Moscow is a very popular event, so you should call in advance for groups and ticket availability. Set extra time aside to discover the museum located at Steamtown. Refer to Chapter 8 for more information about this site.

Hours: April through November: Friday through Sunday, various times of departure. Call for train schedule.

Cost: $10 for adults, $8 for senior citizens, $5 for children ages 15 and under. Inquire about combination ticket prices that include admission to the museum.

Stourbridge Line Rail Excursion   *(717) 253-1960*

742 Main Street
Honesdale, PA 18431

Description: If you think a round-trip from Honesdale to Hawley would be ho-hum, you've never experienced the Stourbridge Line. Ghosts and goblins, Santa and the Easter Bunny have been known to be passengers on the Stourbridge Line and enjoy mingling with their fellow travelers. In the summer, the train seems to get robbed every Sunday. Call the box office during business hours or buy tickets at the visitors center for the ride of a lifetime.

Hours: October: Haunted Train Ride, Fall Foliage Rides. December: Santa Express. March: Bunny Run. Sundays in the summer: Great Train Robbery. Box office is open Monday through Friday, 8:30 a.m. to 4:30 p.m.; Saturday, 9 a.m. to 1 p.m.

Cost: Train rides are $10 for adults and children. The Great Train Robbery is $12 for adults and children.

TROLLEY

Water Gap Trolley   *(717) 476-9766*

PO Box 159
Delaware Water Gap, PA 18327

Description: A one-hour guided trolley ride around the historic Delaware Water Gap is a great way see the area. Your tour guide will tell you all the bits of trivia that make the Poconos unique. You may even get to see the Indian head that is mysteriously carved into the Delaware Water Gap. When you get off the trolley, the fun is not over. Your family will be able to play limitless rounds of miniature golf for $2 per person.

Hours: March through November: daily, 10 a.m. to 4 p.m.

Cost: $5 for adults, $3.50 for children ages 3 to 12, and free for children 2 and under.

GUIDED OR SELF-GUIDED TOURS

Bethlehem Visitors' Center

52 West Broad Street
Bethlehem, PA 18018-5775

(610) 868-1513
(800) 360-8687
♨

Description: The Visitors' Center is a great place to get your footing in Bethlehem. The center offers an orientation film and guided tour of the Moravian district, the Old City Walking Tour, and the 18th-Century Industrial Quarter. This city is transformed with lights and festivities at Christmas time. A trip to Bethlehem during the holiday season will give you the feeling of being in a Dickens village.
Hours: Daily, 9 a.m. to 5 p.m.
Cost: Free.

Covered Bridge Tour

Lehigh Valley Convention and Visitors Center
2200 Avenue A
Bethlehem, PA 18017

(610) 882-9200
(800) 747-0561
♨

Description: Call the Convention Center to get a brochure describing a self-guided tour of the area's covered bridges.
Cost: Free.

Crayola Factory

30 Centre Square
Easton, PA 18042-7744

(610) 515-8000
www.crayola.com/crayola/
👪 ♿ ✍

Description: Your children and the child in you will enjoy this brand-new attraction to the Lehigh Valley. Crayola, the household name for crayons and art supplies, offers a factory-floor tour and several interactive exhibits in the new 20,000 square foot building. Start off with an orientation video of Crayola history, and then roll up your sleeves for coloring, print making, color mixing, sculpting, and using your imagination at the PC Adventure exhibit. This kids wonderland actually has an on-site McDonald's restaurant. This is a definite "must see." Great for school groups, too.
Hours: Tuesday through Saturday, 9:30 a.m. to 5 p.m.; Sunday, 12 noon to 5 p.m. Closed Mondays except for the following

At the Crayola Factory children are encouraged to color outside the lines.
Photo provided by, and reproduced with permission of, Binney & Smith, maker of Crayola products.

federal holidays: Martin Luther King Jr. Day, President's Day, Memorial Day, Labor Day, and Columbus Day.
Cost: $6 for adults and children, $5.50 for senior citizens over 65, and free for children under 2.

East Stroudsburg University Campus Arboretum

(717) 422-3534

Public Affairs Office
East Stroudsburg, PA 18301

⊛ ♦♦♦ ♿

Description: The self-guided walking tour of the East Stroudsburg University campus highlights trees that are either unusual or offer historic significance to the university. The tour is about one mile long and starts at the corner of College Circle and Normal Street. A tour book, which includes a map, can be picked up at the Public Affairs office on campus.

East Stroudsburg University Greenhouse   *(717) 424-3701*

Moore Biology Hall
East Stroudsburg, PA 18301

Description: The University Greenhouse is home to an extensive collection of rare and exotic species of plants. Tours of the greenhouse for small groups must be prearranged.

Lackawanna Coal Mine Tour   *(800) 238-7245*

McDade Park   *(717) 963-MINE*
Scranton, PA 18503

Description: Take a one-hour tour and witness firsthand how coal was harvested. You will travel 300 feet beneath the earth in a mining car, and your personal tour guide will be either a miner or a descendant of a miner. The guide will be able to explain the history as well as convey the tragedies of the mining industry. At the conclusion of the tour each participant will receive an official miners' certificate as a souvenir. Educators will be interested to know that supplemental educational materials are available for your use. Group tours are available by reservation from March through December.

Hours: April through November: 10 a.m. to 4 p.m. Closed Easter and Thanksgiving.

Cost: $6 for adults, $4 for children, and free for children under 3.

Weller Center for Health Education   *(610) 258-8500*

2009 Lehigh Street
Easton, PA 18042

Description: The center presents lectures, exhibits, and audiovisual programs in an effort to promote healthy lifestyles. Nutrition, Family Life, and General Heath are just a sampling of the many programs that are geared for all ages. These presentations are designed for school group tours, although the facility is open to the public on a walk-in basis. Although walk-ins are encouraged, calling ahead is advised.

Hours: Labor Day through mid-June: Monday through Friday, 9 a.m. to 4 p.m. Mid-June through Labor Day: Monday through Friday, 9 a.m. to 2 p.m.

Cost: $2.50 for adults and children.

THE WORLD OF WORK

Any place of work can become an adventure to a child. Most store owners or businesses are happy to explain their jobs and answer questions when the place is not crowded. Use your imagination! The post office, a car wash, bakery, and farms are just a sampling of the dozens of places to explore. The facilities listed here offer guided tours for groups. Arrangements must be made in advance. Tours will be arranged during working hours, and there is no charge for any of the trips listed below.

Blue Ridge Cable
(800) 323-3758

936 Elm Street
Lehighton, PA 18235

Description: Take a tour through the Channel 13 newsroom and control room to see how programs are put together. The highlight of the tour is when the group performs a skit to air on one of the shows the following day. The entire tour takes about 30 minutes to one hour. Call two to three weeks in advance to make arrangements.

Highlights For Children
(717) 253-1164

803 Church Street
Honesdale, PA 18431

Description: The magazine, *Highlights for Children*, has been a part of every child's life. The editorial offices for the first issue of *Highlights for Children* were two rooms over a garage on Main Street in Honesdale. Fifty years later, with a circulation of 2.5 million, *Highlights* has the largest circulation of any children's subscription periodical. Tours of the current editorial facility are available on a walk-in basis. This self-guided tour allows you to see the editorial and art staff working to produce this award-winning magazine. Give a call for further information or group reservations.

Pocono Medical Center
(717) 476-3767

206 East Brown Street   *(717) 476-3766*
East Stroudsburg, PA 18360

Description: The Communications and Media Relations Department will usher small groups on tours of the hospital. The tour will give groups an overview of the hospital environment, and with prior arrangement, the tour will be tailored to suit your group's needs. All tours need to be arranged in advance.

Pocono Record
(717) 421-3000

511 Lenox Street
Stroudsburg, PA 18360   ⊛ ♦♦♦ ♿ ✈

Description: Who? What? When? Where? and How Come? All these questions and more will be answered when you visit the daily newspaper of the Poconos. Contact the paper in advance to arrange a tour.

U.S. Post Office

Anytown, U.S.A.   ⊛ ♦♦♦ ♿ ✈

Description: Most postmasters will grant tours of the post office facility. Scan the blue pages of the phone book for a listing of all the facilities in the area and call in advance to arrange a group tour. The larger the town, the larger the post office, therefore the group may get to see more of the U.S. Postal Service in action.

WSBG-FM/WVPO-AM Radio Station
(717) 421-2100

22 South 6th Street
Stroudsburg, PA 18360   ⊛ ♦♦♦ ✈

Description: Groups will be able to meet the DJs and watch them perform before the microphone. Participants will get to see sound rooms for the Poconos' leading AM and FM stations. If you're lucky, you may even get to say hello to the radio audience. The tour guide will explain how things in the world of radio work and field all questions. Tours need to be pre-arranged.

Pennsylvania Trivia

Before George Washington became the first President of the United States, he made his living netting shad on the Delaware River.

RECOMMENDED READING LIST

FICTION

The books listed below are children's fiction written and illustrated by a couple who reside in the Pocono region with their family. The books depict the natural environment of the Poconos. The pictures as well as the story content will not only educate but entertain the young reader.

Around the Pond: Who's Been Here? by Lindsay Barrett George
Greenwillow Books, $16.00; ISBN: 0-688-14376-8; ages 3 to 8
Picking blueberries turns a warm summer afternoon into an adventure for a brother and sister. Their trip around the pond gives them a chance to see signs of the animals living there. Author's notes give an illustration and narrative of each animal found around the pond.

Beaver at Long Pond by William T. George
Greenwillow Books, $16..00; ISBN: 0-688-07106-6; ages 2 to 7
This story gives the reader a chance to see how a busy beaver spends his day. Find out how these animals build their houses and survive in their watery environment.

Box Turtle at Long Pond by William T. George
Greenwillow Books, $16.00; ISBN: 0-688-08184-3; ages 2 to 7
Spend the day with a box turtle at Long Pond. Find out what he eats, where he sleeps, and how he escapes from a curious raccoon.

Christmas at Long Pond by William T. George
Mulberry Books, $4.95 (paperback); ISBN: 0-688-14731-3; ages 2 to 8
Father and son take a walk on Christmas Eve to find the perfect Christmas tree. Along their journey they see and learn about the animals around them.

Fishing at Long Pond by William T. George
Greenwillow Books, $15.00; ISBN: 0-688-09401-5; ages 2 to 7

While fishing for bass on Long Pond, grandfather and granddaughter pass the time discovering lots of the pond's inhabitants until they hook one.

In the Snow: Who's Been Here? by Lindsay Barrett George
Greenwillow Books, $16.00; ISBN: 0-688-12320-1; ages 3 to 8

On their way to sled, a brother and sister find all kinds of evidence of animal life in the snow. Their trek in the snow ends with a special surprise. The author's notes provide illustrations and narratives of each animal discovered in the snow.

In the Woods: Who's Been Here? by Lindsay Barrett George
Greenwillow Books, $16.00; ISBN: 0-688-12318-X; ages 3 to 8

A walk in the autumn woods for a brother and sister provide an afternoon of fun while learning what animals have been there before them. Telltale signs of animal activities provide clues to the variety of forest inhabitants.

William and Boomer by Lindsay Barrett George
Greenwillow Books: $16.00; ISBN: 0-688-06640-2; ages 2 to 7

In early spring, a little boy and his father find a baby goose. Unable to find its parents, the boy and his family take care of the bird. The story tells of their days together, and how they both learn to swim that summer.

NON-FICTION

This book is a nonfiction account of a sojourn down the Delaware River. Recommended reading for the older child anticipating a canoeing, rafting, or tubing trip.

Voices of the River: Adventures on the Delaware by Jan Cheripko
Boyds Mills Press, $9.95 (paperback); ISBN: 1-56397-622-6; ages 10 and up.

This nonfiction photo journal takes the reader on a 215-mile, 10-day canoe trip from Hancock, NY, down the Delaware River to Philadelphia, Pennsylvania. A good portion of the trip takes place in the Pocono region of the Delaware River.

QUICK GUIDE TO ACTIVITIES

	Page	Birthday Party Facilities	Free Activities	Wheelchair and Stroller Accessible	School Group and Group-Rate Attractions	Rainy Day Activities
CHAPTER 2: ANIMALS						
Apple Tree Farm	36	•		•	•	
Claws and Paws Wild Animal Kingdom	36	•		•	•	
Pocono Snake and Animal Farm	37			•	•	•
Quiet Valley Living Historical Farm	38	•		•	•	
Reptiland	39	•		•	•	•
Trexler-Lehigh County Game Preserve	39	•		•	•	
CHAPTER 3: DEMONSTRATIONS						
Callie's Candy Kitchen	41		•	•	•	•
Callie's Pretzel Factory	42		•	•	•	•
Holley Ross Pottery Factory	42		•	•	•	•
House of Candles	43		•		•	•
CHAPTER 4: HISTORY						
Antoine Dutot School and Museum	45–46				•	•
Asa Packer Mansion	46			•	•	•
Burnside Plantation	46	•	•	•	•	
Bushkill Falls	47				•	
Columns Museum	47				•	•
Driebe Freight Station	47–48			•	•	•
Eckley Miner's Village	48			•	•	•

	Page	Birthday Party Facilities	Free Activities	Wheelchair and Stroller Accessible	School Group and Group-Rate Attractions	Rainy Day Activities
Grey Towers National Historic Landmark	48		•		•	•
Houdini Tour and Magic Show	50	•		•	•	•
Liberty Bell Shrine	50				•	•
Mauch Chunk Museum	50–51				•	•
National Canal Museum	51			•	•	•
Old Jail	51–52				•	•
Pennsylvania Anthracite Heritage Museum	52			•	•	•
Pocono Indian Museum	52			•	•	•
Quiet Valley Living Historical Museum	53			•		
Soldiers and Sailors Monument	54		•			
Stroud Mansion	54				•	•
Wayne County Historical Society Museum	54			•	•	•
Zane Grey Museum	55				•	•

CHAPTER 6: LIBRARIES

	Page	Birthday Party Facilities	Free Activities	Wheelchair and Stroller Accessible	School Group and Group-Rate Attractions	Rainy Day Activities
Barrett Friendly Library	68		•	•		•
Bethany Public Library	71		•	•		•
Clymer Library	68		•	•		•
Delaware Township Library Association	70		•			•
Dimmick Memorial Public Library	67		•	•		•
Dingman/Delaware Branch Library	70		•	•		•
Eastern Monroe Public Library	69		•	•		•
Greeley Branch Library	71		•	•		•
Hawley Public Library	71		•	•		•
Kemp Library	69		•	•		•
Lehighton Memorial Public Library	68		•	•		•
Newfoundland Area Public Library	72		•	•		•
Palmerton Library	68		•	•		•

	Page	Birthday Party Facilities	Free Activities	Wheelchair and Stroller Accessible	School Group and Group-Rate Attractions	Rainy Day Activities
Pike County Public Library	71		•	•		•
Pleasant Mountain Public Library	72		•	•		•
Pocono Mountain Public Library	69		•	•		•
Pocono Township Branch Library	69		•	•		•
Salem Public Library	72		•			•
Smithfield Branch Library	70		•	•		•
Wayne County Public Library	72		•	•		•
Western Pocono Community Library	70		•	•		•

CHAPTER 8: MUSEUMS

	Page	Birthday Party Facilities	Free Activities	Wheelchair and Stroller Accessible	School Group and Group-Rate Attractions	Rainy Day Activities
Allentown Art Museum	75–76			•	•	•
Carbon County Railway Station	76		•	•		•
Dorflinger Glass Museum	76				•	•
Everhart Museum of Nat. History, Science, Art	77			•	•	•
Hooven Mercantile Co. Museum	77				•	•
Jem Classic Car Museum	78				•	•
Kemerer Museum of Decorative Arts	78	•		•	•	•
Kittatinny Point Nature Museum	79		•	•	•	•
Madelon Powers Gallery	79		•	•	•	•
Mary Stolz Doll and Toy Museum	80				•	•
Monroe County Environmental Ed. Center	80		•	•	•	•
Museum of Indian Culture	81	•		•	•	•
Pennsylvania Fishing Tackle Museum	81				•	•
Pocono Museum Unlimited	82			•	•	•
SMART Discovery Center	82			•	•	•

CHAPTER 9: NATURE

	Page	Birthday Party Facilities	Free Activities	Wheelchair and Stroller Accessible	School Group and Group-Rate Attractions	Rainy Day Activities
Carbon County Environmental Ed. Center	86				•	
Delaware Valley Raptor Center	89–90				•	

	Page	Birthday Party Facilities	Free Activities	Wheelchair and Stroller Accessible	School Group and Group-Rate Attractions	Rainy Day Activities
Delaware Water Gap National Rec. Area	91		•	•	•	
Dorflinger-Suydam Wildlife Sanctuary	86		•			
Lacawac Wildlife Sanctuary	87				•	
The Nature Conservancy	88		•		•	
Pennsylvania Raptor and Wildlife Association	90				•	
Pike County Conservation District	88			•	•	
Pocono Environmental Education Center	89		•	•	•	•
Pocono Wildlife Rehabilitation Center	90.				•	

CHAPTER 10: PARKS

	Page	Birthday Party Facilities	Free Activities	Wheelchair and Stroller Accessible	School Group and Group-Rate Attractions	Rainy Day Activities
Camelback Alpine Slide	101	•			•	
Carousel Water and Fun Park	103	•			•	
Costa's Family Fun Park	103	•		•	•	•
Dorney Park and Wildwater Kingdom	103–104	•		•	•	
Fun and Games	104	•			•	•
Go-Kart Rides	104	•		•	•	
Golf Plus Park	105	•			•	
Imagination Zone	105	•		•	•	•
King of Swing	105	•			•	
Pocono Go-Karts	106	•		•	•	
Shawnee Place Play and Water Park	107	•			•	
Thunder Creek Quarry	107	•			•	•
Time Out Family Amusement Center	107	•		•	•	•

CHAPTER 11: PERFORMING ARTS

	Page	Birthday Party Facilities	Free Activities	Wheelchair and Stroller Accessible	School Group and Group-Rate Attractions	Rainy Day Activities
Allentown Symphony Hall	109			•	•	•
Fine Arts and Performing Center	113			•	•	•
Fine Arts Discovery Series	110			•	•	•
FM Kirby Center for Performing Arts	113			•	•	•

	Page	Birthday Party Facilities	Free Activities	Wheelchair and Stroller Accessible	School Group and Group-Rate Attractions	Rainy Day Activities
Kids Express TV Show	113		•			•
Kindermusik Beginnings	110					•
Lehigh Valley Chamber Orchestra	111					•
Little Theater of Wilkes-Barre	114			•	•	•
Mauch Chuck Opera House	114			•	•	•
Music for Little People	111	•		•		•
Northeastern Pennsylvania Philharmonic	111			•	•	•
Pennsylvania Sinfonia Orchestra	112			•	•	•
Pocono Playhouse	114			•	•	•
Presbyterian Church of the Mountain	112		•			
Ritz Co. Playhouse	114			•	•	
Shawnee Mountain Summer Concert Series	112		•			
Shawnee Playhouse	115			•	•	•
State Theater Center for the Arts	115	•		•	•	•
Touchstone Theater	115	•		•	•	•

CHAPTER 12: SPORTS

940 Golf 'N Fun Family Play Park	132	•		•	•	
Adventure Sports	121				•	
Ashley Lanes	128	•		•	•	•
Big Brown Fish and Pay Lake	129	•		•	•	
Big Wheel Family Skating Center	142	•			•	•
Big Wheel North Family Skating Centers	142	•			•	•
Big Wheel Oasis	148	•				
Carson's Riding Stables	130				•	
Casino Theater	133	•		•	•	
Chamberlain Canoes	122				•	
Colonial Lanes	128	•		•	•	•

	Page	Birthday Party Facilities	Free Activities	Wheelchair and Stroller Accessible	School Group and Group-Rate Attractions	Rainy Day Activities
Cypress Lanes	128	•			•	•
Deer Path Riding Stables	130	•		•	•	
Eagle Valley Miniature Golf	133	•			•	
Indian Head Canoe and Raft Trips	122				•	
Jim Thorpe River Adventures	117–118, 125				•	
King of Swing Miniature Golf	133			•		
Kittatinny Canoes	123				•	
Lackawanna County Stadium	146	•		•	•	
Lackawanna Stadium on Ice	140	•			•	
Lehigh Valley Velodrome	118, 146–147		•	•	•	
LeRose's Roller Skating Rinks	143	•		•	•	•
Mountain Creek Riding Stable	131	•		•	•	
Mountain Manor Inn Ice Skating	140	•			•	•
Mystic Pines Miniature Golf	134	•		•	•	
Northeast Sports	118–119				•	
Pack Shack Adventures	123				•	
Pocono Bicycle Tours	119–120			•	•	
Pocono Family YMCA	148, 149	•				•
Pocono Ice-A-Ramas	141	•			•	•
Pocono Lanes	128				•	•
Pocono Whitewater Bike Tours	120				•	
Pocono Whitewater Rafting	125				•	
Rocky Road Miniature Golf	134	•			•	
Scotty's Whitewater Rafting	124–125				•	
Shawnee Roller Skating Rinks	143	•		•	•	•
Sky Lanes	128	•		•	•	•
Triple W Riding Stables	132	•		•	•	

	Page	Birthday Party Facilities	Free Activities	Wheelchair and Stroller Accessible	School Group and Group-Rate Attractions	Rainy Day Activities
Whitewater Challengers Bike Tours	120				•	
Whitewater Rafting Adventures	126				•	

CHAPTER 13: TOURS

	Page	Birthday Party Facilities	Free Activities	Wheelchair and Stroller Accessible	School Group and Group-Rate Attractions	Rainy Day Activities
Back Roads of Monroe County Bus Tour	154				•	•
Bethlehem Visitors' Center	157		•			
Blue Ridge Cable TV Station	160		•		•	
Canal Boat Rides	152–153				•	•
Covered Bridge Tour	157		•			
Crayola Factory	157–158			•	•	•
East Stroudsburg U Campus Arboretum	158		•	•	•	
East Stroudsburg U Greenhouse	159		•		•	
Highlights for Children	160		•		•	•
Lackawanna Coal Mine Tour	159			•	•	•
Moyer Aviation	151–152			•		
Pocono Medical Center	160–161		•	•	•	•
Pocono Record	161		•	•	•	•
Rail Tours	154			•	•	•
Sparta Aviation	152			•		
Spirit of Paupack Scenic Boat Tours	153			•	•	
Steamtown National Historic Site	155			•	•	•
Stourbridge Line Rail Excursion	156		•	•	•	•
U.S. Post Office	161			•	•	•
Wallenpaupack Scenic Boat Tour	153			•	•	
Water Gap Trolley	156				•	•
Weller Center for Heath Education	159			•	•	•
WSBG-WVPO Radio Station	161		•		•	•

INDEX

940 Golf N' Fun Family Play Park, 132

A

Action Sports Marina, 127
Adventure Sports, 121
AJ's Vegetables and Produce, 93
Allentown Art Museum, 75–76
Allentown Symphony Hall, 109
Alpine Mountain Ski Area, 137
Annual Barrett Township Halloween, 63
Antoine Dutot School and Museum, 45–46
Apple Tree Farm, 36
Asa Packer Mansion, 46
Ashley Lanes, 128
Autumn Balloon Festival, 62

B

Back Roads of Monroe County Bus Tour, 154
Barrett Friendly Library, 68
Beltzville State Park, 91, 98
Bertram's Orchard, 95
Bethany Public Library, 71
Bethlehem Musikfest, 61
Bethlehem Visitors' Center, 157
Big Boulder Ski Area, 137; Jack Frost, 135
Big Brown Fish and Pay Lake, 129
Big Pocono State Park, 98
Big Wheel Family Skating Center, 142
Big Wheel North, 142–143
Big Wheel Oasis, 148
Blue Mountain Ski Area, 137
Blue Ridge Cable, 160
Bunnell's Pond Resort, 19
Bunny Run, 58
Burney's Cottages and Motel, 19
Burnside Plantation, Inc., 46
Bushkill Falls, 47

C

Callie's Candy Kitchen, 41
Callie's Pretzel Factory, 42
Camelback Alpine Slide, 101; Ski Area, 137
Canal Boat Rides, 152-153
Carbon County Environmental Education Center, 86
Carbon County Railway Station, 76
Carousel Water and Fun Park, 103
Carson's Riding Stables, Inc., 130
Casino Theater, 73, 133
Celebration of the Arts, 61
Chamberlain Canoes, 122
Chateau at Camelback, 21
Chestnut Lake Campground, 28
Christmas of Olde, 64
Christmas Village, 64
Cinema 6, 73
Claws and Paws Wild Animal Park, 36
Cliff Park Inn, 135
Clymer Library, 68
Colonial Lanes, 128
Columns Museum, 47
Costa's Family Fun Park, 103
Covered Bridge Tour, 157
Cranberry Bog, 88
Cranberry Bog Nature Walk, 59
Cranberry Run Campground, 29
Crayola Factory, 157–158
Cross-Country Skiing Hot Line, 134
Cultural Council, 83
Cypress Lanes, 128

D

Daniels Chestnut Grove Resort, 21
Daniels Top-o-the-Poconos Resort, 21
Dansbury Park Pool, 148
Deer Path Riding Stables, Inc., 130
Delaware Township Library Association, 70

Delaware Valley Raptor Center, 89–90
Delaware Water Gap KOA, 29
Delaware Water Gap National Recreation Area, 91, 100, 101
Delaware Water Gap Pool, 148
Dimmick Memorial Public Library, 67
Dingman/Delaware Branch Library, 70
Dingmans Campground, 29
Don Laine Campground, 29
Dorflinger Glass Museum, 76, 110
Dorflinger-Suydam Wildlife Sanctuary, The, 86
Dorney Park and Wildwater Kingdom, 103–104
Double W Ranch Bed and Breakfast, 18
Driebe Freight Station, 47–48

E
Eagle Valley Miniature Golf, 133
East Stroudsburg University, 146; campus arboretum, 158; greenhouse, 159; theater, 73
Easter Bunny Trail Rides, 58
Eastern Monroe Public Library, 69
Eckley Miner's Village, 48
Evergreen Park Cross-Country Skiing, 135
Everhart Museum of Natural History, Science, and Art, 77

F
Fairway Villas, 27
Fall Foliage Festival, 62
Farm Animal Frolic, 59
Fern Ridge Campground, 30
Fernwood Resort, 23,136, 138
Fine Arts and Performing Center: Theater and Concert Hall, 113
Fine Arts Discovery Series: Concerts for Children, 110
fireworks, 60
FM Kirby Center for the Performing Arts, 113
Four Seasons Campground, 30
Foxmoor Cinemas, 73

Foxwood Family Campground, 30
Free Fishing Day in Pennsylvania, 60
Fun and Games, 104, 133

G
Gap Theater, 74
Go-Kart Rides, 104
Golf Plus Park, 105, 133
Gould's Produce, 94
Gouldsboro State Park, 98
Graver Orchards, 92
Great Pocono Pumpkin Patch Festival, The, 63
Greeley Branch Library, 71
Green-Dreher Sterling Fair, 61
Grey Towers National Historic Landmark, 48

H
Halloween Extravaganza and Parade, 63
Harvest Festival, 63
Haunted Hayrides, 63
Hawley Harvest Hoe-down, 64
Hawley Public Library, 71
Healthy Kids Day, 58
Heckman Orchards, 94
Heller's Farm Market, 94
helpful phone numbers, 14
Hemlock Campground, 30
Hickory Run State Park, 91, 99
Hidden Valley Farms, 94
Highlights For Children, 160
Hillside Lodge, 23
Holley Ross Pottery Factory, 42
Hooven Mercantile Company Museum, 77
Houdini Tour and Magic Show, 50
House of Candles, 43

I
Imagination Zone, 105
Indian Head Canoe and Raft Trips, 122

J
Jack Frost Mountain, 138
Jem Classic Car Museum, 78

Jim Thorpe Camping Resort, 31
Jim Thorpe River Adventures, 117–118, 125

K
Keen Lake Camping and Cottage Resort, 31
Kemerer Museum of Decorative Arts, 78
Kemp Library at East Stroudsburg University, 69
Kens Woods Campground, 31
Kettle Creek Wildlife Sanctuary, 87
Kid Fest, 60
Kids Express TV Show, 113
Kindermusik Beginnings, 110
King of Swing, 105; Miniature Golf, 133
Kittatinny Canoes, 123
Kittatinny Point Nature Museum, 79

L
Lacawac Wildlife Sanctuary, 87
Lackawanna Coal Mine Tour, 159
Lackawanna County Statium, 146
Lackawanna Stadium on Ice, 140
Laurel Blossom Festival, 59
Laurel Festival of the Arts, 59
Lehigh Gorge State Park, 99
Lehigh Valley Arts Council, 83
Lehigh Valley Chamber Orchestra, 111
Lehigh Valley International Airport, 13
Lehigh Valley Velodrome, 118, 146–147
Lehighton Memorial Public Library, 68
LeRose's Roller Skating Rink, 143
Liberty Bell Shrine, 50
Little Theater of Wilkes-Barre, 114
Loft, The, 118
Lyle's Produce, 94

M
Madelon Powers Gallery, 79
Mahoning Drive-In, 74
Maple Sugaring, 57

Maplerock Campsite, 31
Martz Trailways, 13
Mary Stolz Doll and Toy Museum, 80
Mauch Chunk Historical Society, 55
Mauch Chunk Museum, 50–51
Mauch Chunk Opera House, 114
Memorytown, 18
Meesing Site, 87–88
Milford Theater, 74
Monroe County Arts Council, 83
Monroe County Environmental Education Center, 80, 87
Monroe County Historical Society, 55
Monroe County Transit Authority, 13
Montage Mountain Skiing, 138
Mount Tone Ski Area, 138
Mountain Bike Weekend, 60
Mountain Creek Riding Stables, 131
Mountain Laurel Resort, 23–24
Mountain Manor Inn, 140
Mountain Vista Campground, 32
Moyer Aviation, Inc., 151–152
Museum of Indian Culture, 81
Music for Little People, 111
Mystic Pines Miniature Golf, 134

N
Naomi Village, 20
National Canal Museum, 51
Nature Conservancy, The, 74, 88
Nazareth Raceway, 144–145
Nemanie Village, Inc., 20
Newark International Airport, 13
Newfoundland Area Public Library, 72
Newswanger's Tree Farm, 94
Northeast Sports, 118–119
Northeastern Pennsylvania Philharmonic, 111

O
Old Homestead Tree Farm, 92
Old Jail, 51–52
Old Time Christmas, 64

Olde Time Christmas Celebration, 65
Otter Lake Camp, 32
Otto's Camping Resort and RV Center, 32

P
Pack Shack Adventures, Inc., 123
Palmerton Library, 68
Paradise Trout Preserve, 129
Paupack Blueberry Farm, 95
Peck's Pond Bike Rentals, 119; Boat Rental, 123–124; Store, 141
Pennsylvania Anthracite Heritage Museum, 52
Pennsylvania Fishing Tackle Museum, 81
Pennsylvania Learn to Ski Free Day, 57
Pennsylvania Northeast Territory Visitors Bureau, 15
Pennsylvania Raptor and Wildlife Association, 90
Pennsylvania Sinfonia Orchestra, 112
Peterson Ski and Cycle, 119
Philadelphia International Airport, 13
Pike County Conservation District, 88
Pike County Family Fair, 61
Pike County Historical Society, 55
Pike County Public Library, 71
Pine Crest Boat Rentals, 127
Pleasant Mountain Public Library, 72
Pocmont Resort and Conference Center, 24
Pocono Bicycle Tours, Inc., 119–120
Pocono Downs, 147
Pocono Environmental Education Center, 89
Pocono Family YMCA, 148, 149
Pocono Films and Coffee Shop, 74
Pocono Go-Karts, 106
Pocono Ice-a-Rama, 141
Pocono Indian Museum, 52
Pocono Lanes, 128
Pocono Medical Center, 14, 160–161

Pocono Mountain Municipal Airport, 13
Pocono Mountain Public Library, 69
Pocono Museum Unlimited, 82
Pocono Playhouse, 114
Pocono Raceway, 145
Pocono Record, 161
Pocono Snake and Animal Farm, 37
Pocono Township Branch Library, 69
Pocono Vacation Park, 33
Pocono Whitewater Adventures, 125; Bike Tours, 120
Pocono Wildlife Rehabilitation Center, 90
PP and L Lake Wallenpaupack Camping, 33
Presbyterian Church of the Mountain, 112
Promised Land State Park, 92, 100
Pumpkin Patch and Homecoming Festival, 64

Q
Quiet Valley Living Historical Farm, 38, 53

R
Rail Tours, Inc., 154
Reptiland, 39
Ritz Company Playhouse, 114
River Beach Campsites, 33
Rocky Road Miniature Golf, 134

S
St. Patrick's Day Parade, 58
Salem Public Library, 72
Santa Claus Train Rides, 65
Santa Express, 65
Scotty's Whitewater Rafting, 124–125
Scranton Iron Furnaces, 53
Semmel Farm, 92
Shawnee Canoe Trips, 124
Shawnee Inn and Golf Resort, 24
Shawnee Mountain Ski Area, 139
Shawnee Mountain Summer Concert Series, 112

Shawnee Place Play and Water Park, 107
Shawnee Playhouse, 115
Shawnee Roller Skating Rink, 143
Shawnee Stables, 131
Shawnee VillaShare, 27
Shawnee's Northslope/Valley View/Shawnee Villas, 27
Silver Britches Lakeside Resort, The, 24–25
Ski Big Bear, 139
Sky Lanes, 128
Skytop Lodge, 25
SMART Discovery Center, 82
Smithfield Branch Library, 70
Soldiers and Sailors Monument, 54
Sony Theaters, 74
Sparta Aviation, 152
Spirit of Paupack Scenic Boat Tours, 153
Split Rock Lodge and Conference Center, 25–26, 136, 139
Starting Gate, The, 144
State Theater Center for the Arts, 115
Steamtown National Historic Site, 155
Sterling Inn, 19
Stourbridge Line Rail Excursion, 156
Strawberry Festivals, 60
Stroud Mansion, 54
Stroudsburg Pool, 148
Stroudsburg/Pocono Airport, 13
swimming, 148

T
Tanglewood Ski Area, 139
Thunder Creek Quarry, 107
TICA Bus and Taxi, 14
Time Out Family Amusement Center, 107
Tobyhanna State Park, 92, 100
Touchstone Theater, 115
transportation, 13
Trexler-Lehigh County Game Preserve, 39

Tri-State Canoe and Campground, 34
Tri-State Theater, 74
Triple W Riding Stable, Inc., 132

U
U.S. Post Office, 161

V
Villas at Tree Tops and Fairway, The, 27

W
Walker's Tree Farm and Pumpkin Patch, 93
Wallenpaupack Scenic Boat Tour, 153
Water Gap Trolley, 156
Wayne County Fair, 61
Wayne County Historical Society, 55
Wayne County Museum, 54
Wayne County Public Library, 72
Weller Center for Health Education, 159
West End Fair, 61
Western Pocono Community Library, 70
Wheels In-line Skate and Board Park, 144
Whitewater Challengers, Inc., 126; Bike Tours, 120
Whitewater Rafting Adventures, Inc., 126
Wilkes-Barre/Scranton International Airport, 13
Woodloch Pines, 26
WSBG-FM/WVPO-AM Radio Station, 161
WT Family Camping, Inc., 34

Y
Yuletide Celebrations, 65

Z
Zane Grey Museum, 55

ABOUT THE AUTHOR

Photo by Stephen Sobrinsky

Marynell Kelly Strunk is a graduate of Cedar Crest College in Allentown, Pennsylvania. Currently living in the Poconos with her husband and two daughters, she enjoys exploring and researching all the adventures that life in the Poconos has to offer. In addition to writing this book, she is a feature writer for *Family Living* magazine of Northeastern Pennsylvania, a columnist who specializes in family entertainment, and a contributor, writing about outdoor activities for an on-line magazine.